During the War I Rode a Horse

A cheeky story of the 10th Australian Light Horse 1914-1919

Lyle Vincent Murphy

AuthorHouse™
1663 Liberty Drive
Bloomington, IN 47403
www.authorhouse.com
Phone: 1-800-839-8640

First published by AuthorHouse   10/26/2011

ISBN: 978-1-4567-9672-3 (sc)

Printed in the United States of America

Any people depicted in stock imagery provided by Thinkstock are models, and such images are being used for illustrative purposes only.
Certain stock imagery © Thinkstock.

This book is printed on acid-free paper.

Fig. 1. Front cover: The Charge on Beersheba.31ˢᵗ October, 1917
Trooper Herman John Murphy 1916

Contents

Acknowledgements

I would like to acknowledge the people who took the time to read the rough draft of this book and assist in its compilation:

My devoted wife Silvana Murphy.

My brothers, Vernon Murphy and Valmore Murphy.

My sisters, Dulcie Valenti (nee Murphy) and Zita Murphy.

My nephews, Phillip Murphy, David Murphy and Mark Murphy.

My good friend Ben Tennant, who, with his extensive knowledge of computers, created the maps and refined the illustrations.

Introduction

The typical Australian is given to laconic, cryptic, ironical statements. None as ironical as the answer my father gave to my question.

"What did you do during the war, Dad?"

"I rode a horse."

My father, Herman John Murphy, joined the army in World War I on the 19/6/1916. He embarked from Fremantle on *HMAT Lincoln* on the 30/6/1917 and disembarked at Suez, Egypt, on the 6/8/1917. He returned on the *Oxfordshire* as Roll No 308 and disembarked on the 4/8/1919 and was discharged on the 4/9/19.

He saw active service with the 10th Light Horse in the 1st and 3rd machine gun squadron. As part of the Desert Column, he did the 'Long Ride' from Beersheba to Damascus. He served as a Trooper and also served as Acting Corporal and Acting Sergeant at various times without extra pay. This seems to be a typical Murphy trait, doing the work without the pay.

This story is a factional story, which means I have embroidered the facts with fiction to produce an interesting story. In this book I have Herman John Murphy joining the army as a first intake on the 29th of August 1914. The reason for this is to give a picture of the heroism of the Australians in Gallipoli and the events that the men of the

Australian Light Horse experienced. I feel this can be best done by tracking the full course of the war.

Herman's five cousins fought on the Western Front as infantry. All were killed except Charlie Bunter who had his legs cut off exactly where the swagger stick crosses his legs in the photograph *(see Fig. 5)*. In this story I have them as part of the Australian Light Horse in order to provide an example of family closeness and good old Aussie mateship.

Saddle up and enjoy the ride.

Chapter 1: A New Century

The 20th Century began full of promise. It was filled with new inventions and new philosophies. Nationalism was in the air as was imperialism. Nations driven by different principles, morals and visions were striving for supremacy. A single match would start a conflagration. The match was the assassination of Archduke Franz Ferdinand of Austria, heir to the Austro Hungarian thrones and his wife Sophie, Duchess of Hohenburg. The incident took place in the city of Sarajevo on the 28th of June, 1914.

Gavrilo Principe, a member of the group known as Young Bosnia, shot them. The aim of Young Bosnia was the establishment of a Greater Serbia and a break away from Austria-Hungarian rule. Germany came to the support of Austria-Hungary with its intention of annexing Serbia. Russia came to the support of Serbia. France was an ally of Russia and England was an ally of France. So these nations and their dependencies were commonly called the Entente Powers (Allies) and were joined later by Italy and United States.

The Central Powers, so named because of their central location to Europe, consisted of Germany, Austria-Hungary and their associated empires, the Ottoman Empire, which joined the Central Powers in October 1914, followed by Bulgaria a year later.

By the conclusion of the war the only neutral countries were the Netherlands, Switzerland, Spain and the Scandinavian nations.

When Germany advanced into Luxembourg and then Belgium, England declared war on Germany. The official declaration of war was made on the 4th of August 1914.

The Australian press had kept its widespread community well informed. Those who could read followed the events leading up to the declaration of war very closely. Australia did not have a standing army or navy. The country was geared for peace. So with the declaration of war the first new army and navy came into existence.

Recruiting commenced in the major cities of Australia almost immediately. Post cards were sent to every home and large posters were displayed wherever there was a wall.

The Brigadier of the Australian Militia sent letters to his officers inviting them to form regiments on or before the 17th of August 1914. Recruiting commenced on that day in the major cities of each state. On the 29th of August, recruitment began in the country centres.

This was a significant day in the history of the people of Geraldton, a fishing and farming centre four hundred miles north of Perth, the capital of West Australia. It was the day of the Australian Rules Football Grand Final for this district.

Fig 2. Recruiting Postcard

Chapter 2: Into the Fray

"Hey Murph! Will you be able to ruck all the match today?" Bill Fraser called across to Herman Murphy who was leaning over a boot maker's last nailing bars of leather on his work boots. He nailed two bars across the foot of his boot and one across the heel.

"Yeh," was the deep voiced reply from the thickset farmer.

Twenty men were gathered in a corrugated iron shed with a dirt floor preparing for the battle of their lives. It was Saturday the 29th of August 1914.

"Hey Murph are you going to join up?" asked Jack Bunter a cheeky, five foot eight inch rover with blonde hair that covered his twinkling blue eyes.

"Most probably," replied Herman pulling on his boots.

"With a name like Herman you should be fighting for the other side. Isn't Herman a German name? Herman the German," Jack continued to push his luck.

"You could be the first casualty," replied Herman as he flung his boot at his mate who was also his cousin.

"Steady up lads. We've got more important business than the war at the moment," chided Bill Fraser who was both captain and coach of the Chapman Valley Rovers, a football team made up of farmers and railway fettlers from in and around the Chapman Valley. This was rich land, which was watered by the Chapman River and its tributaries twenty miles north of Geraldton. Most of the players for the Rovers were related in some way. Their football jumpers were navy blue with a royal blue chevron at the neck. They were playing against the Geraldton Brigades who drew their players from the fire brigade and the police force. The Brigades wore black jumpers with a red chevron. The teams were competing for the Championship of the 1914 football season.

"Now listen up lads," Bill Fraser said authoritatively.

All the men in the change room went silent as they listened to the wisdom of their coach.

"The team that wins is the one that kicks the most goals. Right?"

"Right!" responded the men in loud agreement.

"We will kick more goals if we go straight down the centre. Right?"
"Right!" the team agreed whole-heartedly.

"Murph takes the knock straight to Jack Bunter. You right Bunts?"

"Right!" responded Bunts with enthusiasm.

"You pass it to me with a low stab pass and I will pass it to Fred Murphy in the full forward. Is that clear Fred?"

"Yep," replied Herman's younger brother.

"Now you know the plan."

"Right!"

"When you go out there I want you to kill the bastards. Give them no mercy. It's kill or be killed. You know the good Christian motto, 'As they would do to you, do you to them but you do it first?' Right?"

"Right!"

"Who are we?" shouted the coach.

A loud resounding roar shook the galvanized walls.

"Rovers!" the men shouted.

"Who are we?"

"Chapman Valley Rovers," again a tin shaking roar from the lads.

"Now let's go out there and get 'em."

With one mighty shout of, "C'arn Rovers," the men charged through the doorway of the change room onto the field.

The field was one hundred and eighty yards long and in the shape of an oval. It was grassed and the grass was cut to a short three inches. At one end of the oval four posts stood glistening white. At the other end a similar set of posts stood. A crowd of supporters surrounded the oval and cheered as the young men ran onto the field in their royal blue and navy blue jumpers, each with a white number on the back. "C'arn Rovers!" was the united chorus from the spectators.

This was Australian Rules football, the greatest game in the universe according to most Australians. It was free, it was wild and it was tough.

The umpire dressed in starched white shirt and shorts blew a shrilled whistle to mark the beginning of the match. He bounced the ball in the middle of the field. A mighty cheer rose from the crowd of football enthusiasts. Herman ran in and leapt high as did an opposing player from the Brigades. Herman punched the ball to his cousin Jack Bunter who 'stab' passed the ball to Bill Fraser playing in the centre half forward position. Bill marked the ball on his chest, turned and kept running. He delivered a brilliant pass to Fred Murphy who had broken away from his defending player. Fred took the mark on his chest. He was some thirty yards from goal, a little to the left of centre, a perfect position for the slender right footer. He kicked a magnificent torpedo punt kick straight though the goal posts. A sprightly young man picked up two flags and signalled a goal while a similar young man at the other end of the oval responded with an identical gesture. The Chapman Valley supporters cheered. The Brigade supporters booed. The ball was taken back to the centre of the field and the ritual was repeated.

The game continued in hearty spirit for twenty-five minutes. Quarter time was called and play ceased for five minutes during which all the players had a drink of water from the same cup attached to a water bag. Blood was wiped from their sweaty faces and the teams changed ends. Again the men chased and tussled and wrestled and fought for the ball so they could kick it through the goal posts or be rewarded with a near miss by kicking it between the point posts. After another twenty-five minutes the game stopped for a fifteen-minute break during which the players had a smoke, a cup of tea and a sandwich. The injury tally was one broken nose, one broken rib, three dislocated fingers and multiple bruises and lacerations for the Rovers and a similar count for the Brigades but all men were prepared to play on. In the second half the intensity increased. The Murphy brothers' combination was lethal.

"Kill him," was the shout from the Brigade supporters as Fred Murphy flew through the air with arms extended. Marking the ball with ease he landed, swivelled on one foot and kicked a goal. The game came down to the last five minutes when the scores were tied. Three quick goals from the Rovers put the grand final in no doubt. Chapman Valley Rovers were the champions for 1914. As the men walked off the field, the recruiting officers for the Army approached them.

"Your country needs you lads. Sign up now."

"Give it a break mate we just finished one war and we won," said Bill Fraser and his team cheered and joined in their team's song *'Chapman Rovers Forever.'*

When the players had changed their clothes and ripped the bars off their work boots, they took the time to listen to the recruiting officers and some did sign up. They then went to the Shamrock Hotel which was on Main Street of Geraldton one mile from the Football Oval to celebrate their victory by drinking copious quantities of beer and re-enacting the game over and over again.

*Fig.3. Chapman Valley Rovers. Herman Murphy lying
on the ground with the football*

"This fellow at footy said someone shot the Archduke of Austria," Fred chimed in.

"Austria? I thought you said the war was with Germany," Elizabeth queried.

"Well the bloke who shot the Archduke of Austria comes from Serbia. He was a member of the Black Hand," Herman explained but knew he wasn't making any sense.

"I got two black hands," joked Jimmy.

"What's it got to do with England anyway?" Elizabeth asked.

"Did you sign up son?" asked Daniel John ignoring Elizabeth's comment.

"Yes," Herman replied.

"When do you leave?" asked Elizabeth.

"Next Wednesday," Herman replied.

"Who else is going?" Daniel John asked.

"Most of the footy team," Herman replied.

"You're not going are you Fred?" Elizabeth asked a little concerned.

"No, I'm too young," Fred replied.

"We'll have to get you ready son," Elizabeth said holding back the tears that would never be shed in public.

The telephone rang.

Daniel John or Jack, as he was commonly known, was the only veterinarian in the valley. Although Jack could not read nor write, he had been granted a Doctor of Veterinary Science by an Act of Parliament. As the law required that only a Doctor of Veterinary Science could practise Veterinary Science and Jack had more knowledge than anyone about curing sick animals, the local governor had thought it appropriate that Jack be allowed to continue his practice. As the vet, he had a telephone connected to the house.

When he returned, he said, "Billy Eastough's filly's got a swollen stomach. He wanted to race her in the Nabawa Cup. I'd better go and fix her up."

"Aren't you going to finish your dinner?" Elizabeth asked.
"I've had enough," said Jack.
"I'll saddle your horse," Herman offered.
"Don't worry big Murph. I'll plurry fix' im up," said Jimmy rising from the table. Jimmy was Jack's virtual shadow.
The meal finished in silence, which was broken by the occasional scrapping of feet on the wooden floor. Dessert was jelly and custard.

After the meal, Michael bade farewell and left in his spring cart for Geraldton. William went to his one room home in the wattle thicket a half a mile down the road.
"Come on son. We'll pack your bag and see if there is any mending to do," Elizabeth said as she left the table. The rest of the family cleared away the dishes.

Fig.4. Chalnooka Homestead 1916

Chapter 4: Black Boy Hill

The railway line, which ran from Yuna to Geraldton, went through the Murphy property. The Yetna Station that was no bigger than an outhouse, was also on the Murphy property and at 10.00 am, Tuesday 2nd of September Herman was there with his family. The small steam train with its rowdy bunch of Chapman Valley recruits pulled into the station. The recruits shouted from the windows of the carriages.

Herman boarded the train with five of his cousins, Charlie Bunter, Jack Bunter, Mick McGuiness, Bill McGuiness, and Ben Murphy. The crowd of some forty souls, who had come to see the future soldiers off, were busily gossiping and the younger children were playing chasey, hide and go seek or having a quiet 'dob of the footy'. No one really knew the significance of either the war or what disasters lay ahead. Most thought the boys were off on a trip to Perth. To them that was far, far away.

The little engine puffed along and collected recruits from the five stations it passed on its way to Geraldton. Here they boarded the big train for Perth. Most of the boys had their clothes and toiletries that consisted of a razor, for those who shaved, a tooth brush and a cake of velvet soap, in a gunny sack which was tied at the neck and toe with a piece of rope and slung over the shoulder. At Geraldton station, officers counted and checked off the names of their recruits. With several confident huffs and puffs, the steam engine pulled its load of enthusiastic lads on a ten-hour journey to Perth. The first hour was noisy and then the rhythm of the train and the onset of darkness lulled the boys to sleep.

At Mingenew the train stopped to take on water. The men got out to stretch their legs and have a quiet smoke. With 'clickety clacks' and the occasional 'whoo hoo' the train hit a breath taking speed of forty miles per hour. The engine driver delighted in sounding the whistle every time he went through a town, which consisted of no more than five houses and a general store.

"I love having revenge on the roosters," he joked with his fireman who kept the furnace roaring.

With an exhausted 'shhhhh' the train stopped at Midland Junction. "Bloody good time," said the stationmaster as he looked at his pocket watch. It was 6.00 in the morning on Wednesday the 3rd of September.

"We're here," Bill Fraser said, as he opened the door of the carriage.

"I can't see any Germans," quipped Jack Bunter as he stepped onto the station.

"You'll see plenty of them in good time," said Major Kevin Maloney who was a teacher from the militia and had been invited to form a regiment.

"Line up lads," he called.

It was a motley lot that met his eye. These were the boys from the bush who had known freedom from birth. The only discipline they had was the discipline of the seasons and hard work. Most had been born to the saddle and could swing an axe from sun up to sun down. They could bend their back over sheep and take off the 'Golden Fleece' all day until the flock was shorn. They were their own masters but would die for mates and family. Kevin Maloney knew this. Although only twenty-five he had taught in the country and knew the calibre of its people.

The three hundred men formed into pairs and marched in a sauntering way to Black Boy Hill three miles east of Midland Junction railway station. Black Boy Hill was a native bush land occupied by wattle trees, small gum trees and lots of Yakka trees which West Australians called Black Boy trees because of their distinctive black trunk. A large area of the bush had been cleared and instead of gum trees there were lines of white, square, canvas tents. City recruits who had already been in residence since The 17th of August greeted the men.

"It was just a bush when we got here. The first few nights we slept under the gum trees until the tents arrived," Corporal Leo Barry explained as he led his group of twelve recruits through the line of tents.

"Well this is it," he continued. "Six in this tent and six in that tent. This is tent 13 Chapman Lane and that one is tent 14."
The men looked at a pile of hessian, foldable beds next to a stack of blankets, mattresses and pillows.
"Unpack the beds and make them. You can get a packing case outside the mess tent. They make excellent bedside tables. Breakfast

is usually at 7.00 am but we've held it over to eight so you guys can settle in," explained the young Corporal.

"Where's the shit house?" Jack Bunter asked.

"In the bush. A wattle and daub shed. Just follow your nose and the flies," responded Corporal Barry.

While Bunts relieved himself in the pit toilets, the men arranged their sleeping quarters. Herman was in tent 13 with Bill Fraser, and his cousins Jack Bunter, Ben Murphy, Mick McGuiness, and Danny O'Dea who made up the six. The adjoining tent had Herman's two cousins Charlie Bunter, Bill McGuiness, Tommy Bray. Richie Burgess, Les Barndon and Mick Siveright made up the rest of group.

Breakfast consisted of scrambled eggs on toast, lashings of bacon and fried tomatoes washed down with a mug of piping hot tea. Geoffrey Dick, commonly called Dicky, was the chef. He was a shearer's cook and had a firm belief that an army marched on its stomach.

"The Q store only opened two days ago. Up to then we wore the clothes we came in," Corporal Barry explained as he took his twelve recruits to be fitted with their uniforms. They were given boots, socks, trousers, tunic, hat, shirts, putties, belt and flannel underwear.

The men had an easy day and took time to get to know each other and their camp. The corporals attached to each group explained the routines. After lunch a cricket bat appeared and several footballs. It wasn't long before several cricket matches were underway. Good old 'tippy run' for the cricketers and simple 'kick to kick' satisfied the football lovers. Evening meal concluded the first day in their new life.

At five the next morning the bugle called out, *"You've got to get up; you've got to get up. You've got to get up in the morning."*

"It's still dark," squawked Jack Bunter.

Bill Fraser up ended his bed. "No slackers in this tent," he said. No one had ever seen Bill Fraser smile. He was always dead serious.

Dressed in shirt, trousers held up by braces, socks, boots and putties, in varying degrees of disarray, the four hundred raw recruits stood on the parade ground. The occasional rabbit and kangaroo had retreated to a safe distance, the magpies warbled to the rising sun and the kookaburras laughed while the white cockatoos chatted amongst themselves in a nearby dead gum tree.

The Prussian manual for training soldiers had been written in 1860. It was solid and the only one available, so the drill sergeants went to work to turn the boys from the bush and city into a fighting unit.

From five thirty to six thirty, it was physical fitness drill and a five-mile jog.

Seven o'clock was breakfast. Dicky ensured it was a hearty breakfast.

Eight o'clock was tent inspection.

Eight thirty combat drill commenced.

"Fix bayonets!" the drill sergeant barked. "Now we want three actions. Action one: hit 'em under the chin. Action two: shove your bayonet in. Action three: put your foot on 'em and pull your bayonet out."

"That's a bloody chaff bag up there Sarg. I'm not sure my foot will reach," Jack Bunter questioned the command.

"Improvise lad, improvise. Now ready. First squad! Charge!"

The men from tent thirteen and fourteen charged. With the butt of the rifle they whacked the chaff bag filled with saw dust hanging from a timber structure very much like an inverted U, then drove the eighteen inch bayonet attached to the 303 rifle into the bag. They simulated putting their foot on it and pulling it out. They then charged onto the next and the next until all twelve bags had been well and truly killed. They returned to the point of origin and commenced again. They were then taken through a series of hand-to-hand combat techniques working in pairs.

Lunch was a welcome break. After lunch there was practice at the rifle range. Most of the country lads were good shots. Most could bring down a rabbit at two hundred yards with a 22 rifle. Hitting a stationary target at two hundred yards was easy. In pairs they practised with their machine guns. One pulled the trigger the other fed the bullets. Evening meal was taken at 6.00 pm and at 9.00 pm all lights were out.

The routine removed any thought of being homesick. At the beginning of the second week, at morning parade, the men were introduced to the horses.

"Most of you will be infantry but we have news that we will be part of the Light Horse battalion. Within the next week we will be selecting those who are competent enough to be members of the Light Horse."

The test was simple. Mount the horse, ride it through an obstacle course of jumps, turns and leaps and then return. To pass, the recruit had to stay on the horse and return.

All the Chapman Valley boys had been riding horses before they could walk. The Perth city boys were not so good. Some got on one side and fell off the other much to the laughter of the assembled throng. Some city slickers went in the right direction but failed to return. They were eventually pursued and collected by a competent rider.

For six weeks intensive training was conducted and the men came together as a unit.

On the 15th of October leave passes were issued.

"Why don't we go and get a studio photograph taken of us all?" asked Ben Murphy.

"Do you mean the whole battalion?" Bill McGuiness asked.

"No just we cousins. The six of us," explained Ben Murphy.

"I am not sure I want to be taken with you ugly buggers," said Charlie Bunter polishing his swagger stick.

"It's a great idea," said Herman. "But where? I've never been to Perth."

"I know the very place," said Charlie Bunter. He worked for Goldsborough Mort and was a regular visitor to Perth. He was quite a handsome lad and fancied himself as a ladies' man.

The lads travelled by train to Perth, a mere fifteen-mile train trip. They had money to spend as they had been paid six shillings a day, which made them the highest paid soldiers in the whole of the allied forces. Herman had elected to collect only a third of his wage and had the rest deposited in the Commonwealth Bank. They arrived at

Perth station at three in the afternoon. Herman was astounded by the size of the station and when he walked into Wellington Street he could not believe the size of the buildings and the amount of traffic.

"Down here," said Charlie Bunter who walked as if he owned the world with his swagger stick under his arm.

They went into the Kodak studios. The studio photograph was taken without any damage to the camera. The photographer assured them the prints would be ready in a week's time.

"Now what are we going to do?" asked Mick McGuiness, who was a man of action.

"I'm going to find a pub and have a few drinks," chirped Jack Bunter.

"I'm with you," harmonized Bill McGuiness and Ben Murphy.

"I've got a date," said Charlie Bunter. "Do you want to come, HJ?"

"I would be in the way," Herman protested.

"No you won't. I'm meeting two sisters at five thirty at the Perth railway station on platform two."

Embarrassing taunts and banter followed which caused Herman to turn red.

"A man has to be introduced to the finer things in life," bragged Charlie. "Come on Murph let's not associate with those country bumpkins. Let's go serve God and Country."

"Strike and strike quickly," they all shouted the 10th Light Horse motto as they parted.

Fig.5. Photograph of the six cousins.
Back Left to right. Ben Murphy, Jack Bunter, Mick McGuiness.
Front Left to right. Herman Murphy, Charlie Bunter, Bill McGuiness.

Chapter 5: Iris Annie Reardon

"There they are," Charlie Bunter said, indicating the two young ladies sitting on the seat on platform two.

"I'll take the short, chubby one," said Herman. The chubby one was not very chubby but next to her sister, who was very thin, she looked chubby. She was, however, as pretty as a picture.

"Hello. My name is Herman Murphy, and this is my cousin Charlie Bunter," the tall trooper said confidently.

Charlie was taken aback at Herman's unusual forthrightness.

"I am Iris Annie Reardon and this is my sister Mary Reardon," Iris greeted the two soldiers who looked very dashing in their dress uniform.

Charlie had met Mary earlier. She worked in the Perth Office of Goldsborough Mort, which handled most of West Australia's wool export.

Opposite Perth station, next to the large department store, Boans, was a boutique tea and cake shop called Rosie's. Most shops closed at five thirty but Rosie's stayed open until eleven in the evening and served many a late carouser with the most delicious cakes and freshly brewed Bushels' tea.

"You can travel a whole day on a cup of Bushels'," Rosy would say as she served her customers.

After a cuppa and cake at Rosie's, the foursome went to the Grand Ballroom, which was on the other side of Boans. Here they danced the waltz, the barn dance, the military two-step, the quick step and swing, the pride of Erin and many other popular dances of the day. After the dance, the soldiers walked their ladies to the tram on Wellington Street. Herman kissed Iris goodnight and said, "You are my little flower" and arranged to meet her next weekend, same time and same station.

The boys arrived back at the Perth station in time to catch the last train to Midland, which left at midnight. They were greeted by a sorry sight.

All of their cousins were drunk. Jack Bunter was singing some inarticulate song. Mick McGuiness was challenging anyone and everyone for a race down the station declaring he was the fastest sprinter in the West, which he probably was. Bill McGuiness was earbashing a poor old stranger telling him how he was going to defeat Germany by himself. Big Ben Murphy was leaning against a post giggling to himself.
The midnight special took the boys to their barracks.

Fig.6. Herman Looking Suave

Fig. 7. Iris Reardon with her brother David Reardon

Chapter 6: The Departure

Before war was declared, England had asked her colonies what their intent would be in case of war. "We will fight to the last man and the last shilling to support mother England," declared Andrew Fisher, the Prime Minister of Australia, 1908 to 1915. And pay they did. The war cost Australia about 24 million pounds which they paid within ten years. Every round, every ship, every bus ride, Australia paid. Mother England even charged for burials and troop transport hire. The number of men who volunteered was 416,809 of which 331,000 served overseas, this was half the male population of these 61,720 died and 155,000 were wounded.

Every available ship was refitted to carry troops from New Zealand and Australia to England where the troops would be retrained at Stonehenge before going to the Western Front. There were delays in departure because several German cruisers were lurking in the waters through which the troop ships had to pass. All ships bearing troops, horses and supplies made their way to King George's Sound just off Albany in West Australia. They began assembling on the 4th of October 1914. Australia had no navy as such so a lot of the ships were commandeered. A white square was painted on the bow and a number was placed in the square to identify the vessel. The ships took it in turn to birth at the small wharf of Albany, take on supplies and allow the men leave. The men on leave would travel by train to Perth, which was about a ten-hour train journey.

The ships that formed the first convoy were as follows. The *Milliades* carried the reserves from the British Army, the *Argyllshire* carried the artillery, *Afric* carried the First Battalion and First Company of Field Engineers and the *Suffolk* carried the Second Battalion. *Clan Maccorquolade* was laden with horses with one man to tend five horses. The *Star of Victoria* carried the First Light Horse regiment. The *Euripides* had the First Infantry Brigade, Third and Fourth Battalions and the First Field Ambulance. The commandeered Orient Liner, *Orviete*, carried General Bridges and the First Australian Divisions, Fifth Battalion and the Second Filed Companies. The *Geelong* brought troops from Tasmania and collected troops from Adelaide.

Other ships included the *Minotaur, Philomel, Pyranees, Melbourne* and the *Wiltshire* as well as the Japanese vessel *Ibaki*; all together there were thirty six transports and three escorting cruisers. A total of 30,000 men and 7843 horses formed the first convoy.

The First Division consisted of:

New South Wales First Infantry Battalions 1-4

Victoria Second Infantry Battalions 5-8

Queensland, West Australia, South Australia and Tasmania formed the 3rd Brigade which was made up of the 9th Battalion from Queensland, 10th Battalion from South Australia, 11th Battalion from West Australia and 12th Battalion was a mixture with men drawn from Tasmania, West Australia and South Australia.

Each battalion consisted of 1023 men.

The 3rd Australian Light Horse Brigade included the 10th Light Horse Regiment in the 1st Division. All of the 10th were drawn from West Australia. Herman was in the 10th Light Horse.

On the 28th of October the troops were on the parade ground at Black Boy Hill. They marched to Midland Junction railway station and boarded the train, which was bound for Albany. The train stopped at Perth to allow the troops to farewell their loved ones.

Herman stood tall in his uniform and sported the slouch hat with the distinctive emu feathers of the Australian Light Horse. There on platform number two stood Iris, in a cute navy dress with white dots, which was adorned with a lace collar.

"Don't you look smart?" she greeted Herman.

"So do you," he replied. Within half an hour the whistles of the squadron leaders were blown and the order, "All aboard," was given.

"I will write," Herman promised.

"So will I," replied Iris. "I will be waiting for you when you return."

"I will return," he said.

"Will you wear this for me?" she asked and passed him a gold ring set with a milky moonstone.

"I will," he said and slipped the ring on his ring finger.

The train pulled out of the station to the sounds of *'Pack Up Your Troubles in Your Old Kit Bag,'* sung by the soldiers who leaned out of the windows of the carriages. Within no time the train had gained speed and the houses and trees and stations flicked past as the train hit its top speed of sixty miles per hour.

Herman, Bill Fraser, Tommy Bray, Richie Burgess, Les Barndon, Mick Siveright and Danny O'Dea were assigned to the *Clan Maccorquolade* and had to assist load more horses onto the vessel. The seven lads were assigned to the same cabin, which was to be their home for the next forty days. They slept in bunks.

On the 1st of November at 6.25 am the first vessel slipped out of King George's Sound. At ten and a half knots, the convoy made its way to Colombo for refuelling and then on to Suez. The horses were corralled on five decks with two below the water line and three above the water line. Each day the horses had to be exercised and have their stable cleaned. On such a journey it was usually expected that twenty per cent of the horses would die for one reason or another. The Australian carers looked on horses as companions. On this journey only three per cent were lost.

Chapter 7: Cairo Bloody Cairo

Turkey joined forces with Germany and declared war on Britain on the 11th of November 1914, and called it a Holy War. The strategy was to get all the Muslim colonies not to support Britain. It did not work, as the Muslims in the British Empire remained loyal to Britain. All this happened while the troop ships from King George's Sound were at sea. The convoy had originally been destined for Wiltshire near Stonehenge in England. Here the men would be trained by the British experts and be prepared to take their positions in the Western Front. But things were not quite ready.

The influx of Canadians had created accommodation chaos and a shortage of supplies. So short were the supplies that the volunteers trained with broomsticks instead of rifles. A resounding, *'Bang! Bang! You're dead,'* was undoubtedly sufficient to kill the enemy on the training grounds but not sufficient in the reality of the battlefield. This, together with Turkey joining the war, caused the British War Cabinet to divert the First Australian Division to Egypt.

"So this is bloody Cairo?" whined Jack Bunter as he walked down the gangplank onto the wharf at Suez on the 15th of December 1914.
"No this is Suez," said Charlie Bunter.
"Cairo is a 'coupla' miles that way," said Ben Murphy pointing west.
"Well it's bloody hot I can tell you," replied Bunts, not to be out done and then lined up in parade formation on the wharf.
"This is the winter," said Richie Burgess.

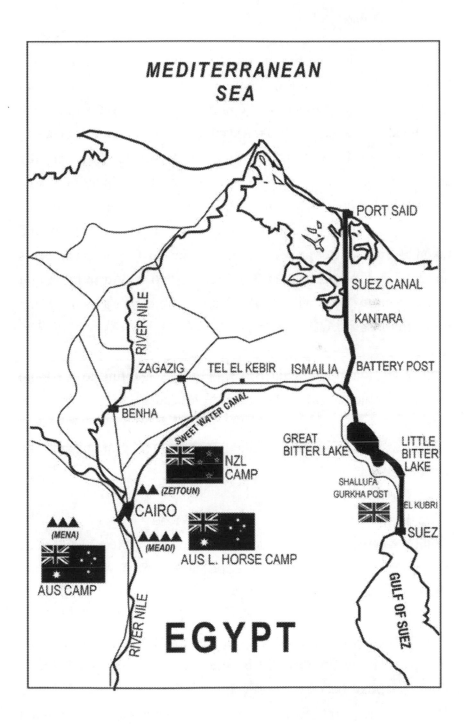

Fig. 8. Egypt and the Suez Canal

The Australian Battalions were sent to three sites around Cairo. Each Australian Light Horse Regiment was commanded by a lieutenant colonel and each regiment was composed of three squadrons each commanded by a major. The largest camp was near Mena, the second further out at Moascar, and the third was at Meadi a pleasant little suburb on the banks of the Nile. Excellent water supplies and large areas, which were easily fenced off made these places ideal for the Light Horse. The men and horses were disembarked at Suez and taken by train to their respective camps. The New Zealand engineers and artillery went to Zeitoun, The infantry and the Australian Light Horse went to Mena and Meadi. Each of the camps was about ten miles from Cairo.

"Those are Pyramids," said Bill McGuiness pointing to the large triangular structures rising from the desert sands.

"What do you do in them?" asked Jack Bunter squinting into the setting sun.

"You die in them," said Ben Murphy who read a book once.
"That's where the ancient rulers of Egypt are buried," said Mick McGuiness who knew a little more about the world beyond Chapman Valley.

The camp was just a sandy desert. It adjoined a new residential area that had been developed by the English Public Service, and although it had been started seven years before it was still in the developmental stage. No provision had been made for ten thousand Australian soldiers and just as many horses. The camp site was a mere half a mile from the Meadi railway station so transport from

Suez to the camp site was easy but there were no tents or buildings on the camp site.

"You'll just have to make do until our equipment arrives," their commanding officer directed as the men looked vacantly at the sand dunes in front of them.

Several of the troopers had brought along pet kangaroos as mascots. Others had bought gum tree seedlings, hoping to create a home away from home.

"We could have kangaroo stew for tea," suggested Ben Murphy and civil war almost started between Victoria and West Australia.

On the first night in camp the men contented themselves with bush biscuits and black billy tea. They slept on their ground sheets and used their greatcoats for blankets.

The disembarkation of the horses began as soon as the men had been transported to their various campsites. The smell of fresh warm air seemed to fill the horses with newfound energy after being cooped up in the ships stables for so long. The journey had sapped their energy and they were in no condition for riding for at least three weeks.

"Take it easy lad," Herman whispered into the ear of his chosen mount as he led the eighteen hands chestnut down the ramp with four other horses obediently following. He had named his horse Peter, a gelding from Albany. Tether lines and feed troughs had been prepared for the horses by the time they reached Meadi on the 12th of December.

"Bloody hell Murph you smell like a stable hand," said Charlie Bunter as he strode up behind his cousin. Herman was pouring oats into the canvas feed troughs.

"I've been sleeping with some very good company lately. This is Peter, Star, Flour, Thunder, Mosquite and Kaiser Bill. Meet my cousin Mick," Herman introduced his line of horses to his cousin. The horses snorted a greeting.

"Glad to meet you mate," Herman said as he shook his cousin's hand and they walked off to renew acquaintances with old tent 13 and 14.

"I gave you guys two days to get the tents ready and all I can see is bare ground. What's the story?" Herman asked.

"Our supplies are not due for a couple of weeks so we have to make do," Bill Fraser explained.

"What about the town?" Herman asked indicating the British suburb of Meadi, "Surely they have something?" Meadi was under the jurisdiction of the London based Egyptian Delta Land and Investment Company. Most of the residents were British except for a few Germans who on the declaration of war were automatically considered aliens and their goods and houses were confiscated by the British Government. Most of the Meadi Brits were glorified administrators in the employ of the Egyptian government.

As the sun began to set in a blaze of orange across the western desert, the boys from Chapman Valley dwindled off to the building sites of Meadi. They moved off in threes so as not to draw too much attention.

"If it is not nailed down and it can be of use to us we bring it home. We are sleeping in luxury tonight," Bill Fraser explained.

"Isn't that stealing?" asked Tommy Bray innocently with his slouch hat sitting on the back of his head and his thick blonde curly hair blowing in the evening breeze.

"This is bloody war son. It isn't stealing. It is army requisitioning," Jack Bunter spouted out as a true blue officer in the British Army would. Satisfied, the men set out on their mission. These were the Bedouins from Australia.

The early morning sun spread its light across the camp. Amidst the hundreds of lumps of greatcoats stood two magnificent edifices. They were not quite up to the standard of the pyramids but they would have put the best of Bedouin tents to shame. The Chapman boys could make an outhouse out of a couple of chaff bags so they had no difficulty whatsoever in constructing a couple of liveable tents from materials acquisitioned from the building sites of Meadi. The floors of the tent were well carpeted and cushioned. The black tents were stretched across some very classy pine joists. Sturdy straining ropes kept the tents in position with well-dressed tent pegs driven into the sandy soil with elegant sledgehammers. Not to be outdone the remainder of the men of the 10th Light Horse followed suit the next night. With the arrival of supplies it was not long before a tent city had grown just a little south of the neatly manicured suburb of Meadi, which the Aussies called the Garden City.

Such army acquisitioning behaviour did eventually bring about a series of 'dos and don'ts' for the Aussies from the neighbouring British.

"Of what use is it?" asked a British bureaucrat as signs were posted on the wall of the hotel adjoining the Meadi railway station. "Those

Aussies can't even speak English so I am quite sure they can't read it."

They could read but they had a habit of ignoring orders.

On the 19th of December 1914 the British deposed the Turkish appointed Khedive of Egypt and declared Egypt a British Protectorate. The Turks hoped the idea of a holy war would produce a series of riots in Egypt following the takeover but the riots never came. For the men in camp Meadi, however, other things were on their minds.

The men soon settled into a heavily scheduled routine. The horses had to be groomed, fed and exercised every day. There was to be no riding until the horses had gained their strength after the long boat ride. This took the best part of four weeks.

"Hey Les give us a hand," Herman called to Les Barndon. "You can come too Richie." Both Richie Burgess and Les Barndon were in tent fourteen and had risen early to put on the billy.

"What are you up to now Murph?" asked Les Barndon. He was always smiling in a giggling way. He was not tall, only around the five foot eight mark but he was both a magnificent swimmer and a tenacious runner. He played in the back pocket for the Chapman Valley Rovers.

"It's Christmas mate and we need a Christmas tree. If we are fast enough we should be able to get one before any wise men know about it."

Richie Burgess was a tall, handsome son of the retired magistrate of the Chapman Valley area. He lived on a small farm with his parents and had planned to follow a career in Law for some unknown reason. He was at times quite vague.

"It is only the twenty third," he said in his educated Australian accent. "We have two days to go."

"Come on," Herman responded ignoring the comment.

Herman walked out of the campsite and along the Khashab Canal, which was the eastern flank of the camp and into the fringe of Meadi. The street had a line of green Norfolk pines on each side of the broad street. With four deft swings of the axe that he was carrying Herman fell the tree.

"Our Christmas tree gentlemen," Herman said.

With Herman in the front, Richie Burgess in the rear and Les Barndon in the middle the three men carried the tree back to camp humming *'We Three Kings of Orient Are'* in muted tones. They buried the base three feet into the ground. It stretched twenty foot into the sky.

"Nice," said Jack Bunter as he walked around the tree inspecting it while drinking his early morning cuppa.

"The *pommy* ordinance sergeant complained about our wasting jam tins. We can hang the tins on the tree as decorations," he added.

The men decorated the Christmas tree with jam tins, bottles, old socks, which had been dutifully washed, and any pieces of coloured cloth they could find. The cloth was tied into delicate bows.

Danny O'Dea and Ben Murphy had made a Christmas cake which was no more than sweet damper filled with dates, sultanas, apricots and lots of orange and lemon peel. It was cooked in a camp oven that had somehow come into the possession of tent 13.

On Christmas Eve just after sundown the men lit a large campfire and gathered around. The men drank sweet hot tea laced with good old Bundaberg rum and sang Christmas carols. Danny O'Dea had an outstanding tenor voice and knew more than the first line of most of the popular carols so he led the singing. Mick McGuiness and Mick Siveright both played a raunchy mouth organ. There were piano accordions, trumpets, fiddles and improvised instruments that made up the musical ensemble. Danny rounded off the evening with *Ave Maria, Danny Boy* and finally *Silent Night.* Father Flanagan celebrated midnight mass, with the ministers of other denominations sharing the sermon time.

"That was really nice," said Jack Bunter as he rolled over on his cushioned bed. "Really nice." He pulled his great coat up to his chin to keep out the cold and slept. War was not on the minds of the 10th. This was a time of "Peace on Earth and Goodwill to all Mankind" and mates.

The Christmas supplies from Australia, destined for the men overseas, never arrived so Christmas dinner was an improvised affair. The goat on the spit outside tent 13 sent its delicious aromas through the rest of the tents.

"It wandered into the camp and offered itself up as the sacrificial lamb," Bill McGuiness explained to Major Maloney innocently. His chubby cheeks turning into two little red apples as he grinned. The Major joined the boys for Christmas dinner.
"It's a bit chewy but quite palatable," he spoke of the Christmas cake as he reached for a second slice. "What treat do you have in store for us for New Years Day?"
"A bit of a surprise Major," Herman tantalized his commanding officer, "but I think you will enjoy it."

"I can hardly wait," he replied as he stood up and thanked the men for the dinner and continued to his quarters in the hotel near the Meadi railway station.

By New Years Day the horses were ready for a full work out so the boys of tent 13 and 14 had decided to hold an unofficial race meeting. The track was straight to ensure no excessive strain would be put on the horses' legs.
It was straight down the main street of Meadi.

"It's a perfect mile," Herman explained. He was clerk of course and sat proudly astride Peter. His dress uniform was well groomed and his slouch hat with a cockade of emu feathers sat squarely on his head. The road was wide enough for a field of six horses. Jack Bunter, Mick McGuiness and Mick Siveright ran the betting ring. Bill Fraser, Tommy Bray and Richie Burgess took the registrations. Les Barndon and Danny O'Dea were the starters. They had organized the bugler to call the horses for each race. Ben Murphy, Bill McGuiness and Charlie Bunter had organized the drinks, which consisted of beer and beer and more beer. Several outsiders were judges. Signallers were at work to carry messages from the judges to the starters. It was a well-organized fixture. Several members of the artillery organized games of 'two up' around the course.

The first race commenced right on time at 10.30 am and the rest followed every forty minutes. The final race was due to start at 3.10 pm. However at 3.00 pm a Rolls Royce drove into Meadi. The elite car stopped on the fringe of the city because the main street was blocked with the racing event and each side of the street was crowded with soldiers and locals all shouting and drinking and cheering and laughing. The driver dressed in British army uniform and wearing the insignia of a major got out of the car and opened the door for the dignitary in the back seat. The dignitary stepped out. He was the dapper fifty-year-old General Sir George William Birdwood who was not amused with the behaviour of the soldiers.

"Major! What is going on here?" he asked his aide de camp.

"I shall ask," replied the major.

The major walked among the men expecting to receive recognition of his rank in the form of standing at attention or a salute. With nothing of the kind forthcoming, he approached one of the judges.

"Excuse me trooper, what is going on?" asked the major in superior tones and an Eton College accent.

"Eh?" responded Jimmy Clark a butcher from Perth." You wanna know what's goin' on. Are ya blind mate? It's a bloody race meeting and if you don't move you'll be run down by six horses coming lickity split down the track in exactly ten minutes."

"Sir! Do you know to whom you are speaking?" replied the major offended by the brash manner of the colonial soldier.

"No mate but my name is Jimmy Clark from Perth. You're a *pommy bastard* aren't you? I can tell by your way of talkin'. If you're quick, you could get a couple of shillings on Lightning. He's bound to win this race."

Realising he was getting nowhere the major turned on his heels and returned to the Rolls and spoke to the general.

"It is a race meeting, Sir. And may I say these Australian troops are a disgrace to the uniform, Sir. They have no breeding, no discipline and have no idea of military protocol. Apparently if we don't get off the road we will be run down by a group of horses which will be coming down the main street in about five minutes."

General Sir William Birdwood assessed the situation and decided to retreat.

"Driver! Let's go back to the officers' quarters. I believe they have taken up residence in the Hotel adjoining the Meadi Railway Station. We should be in time for a gin and tonic."

General Sir William Birdwood was not a patient man. He had been waiting in the Hotel Lounge for three hours. So when the Australian officers returned to headquarters at the Meadi Hotel, having spent a delightful day at the race meeting, the General launched his barrage.

"I want all of the men and officers on the parade ground at seven hundred hours. I will expect them fully uniformed with backpacks ready for exercise. The horses seemed quite disciplined but the men are not. Now take me to my quarters."

The ants' nest had been stirred.

The Meadi tennis courts were used as a parade ground. The men were lined up and underwent an inspection. Each had a backpack, a rifle and two bandoliers of bullets, which carried ninety rounds each

"What are you wearing, trooper?" General Birdwood asked Jack Bunter as he looked him directly in the eye.

"Ha, shirt, trousers, boots," was the proud reply.

"What has happened to the bottoms of your trousers?"

"Aw. I cut the legs off. They are cooler that way," Bunts replied.

General Birdwood stretched to his full five foot six inches, sucked in his breath and spat out his words.

"You will get a further issue of trousers and if you tamper with them in any way you will be court marshalled."

41

"Keep your shirt on Sir. It's only a bloody pair of trousers and it's hot out here."

The General moved on and stopped in front of Herman.

"Trooper! Are you aware your shirt has no sleeves?" he asked.

"Yes sir. I ripped them off. I feel cooler with my shirt sleeves off," Herman replied respectfully.

"You will sew them back on by tomorrow morning," the British officer commanded.

"I've been using the sleeves as oiling rags for my saddle," Herman replied respectfully.

"Well get another shirt!"

After the parade the men were dismissed. Sir General William Birdwood held a staff meeting.

"It is my duty to mould the Australian and New Zealand forces stationed here in Egypt into a fighting force to protect the Mother Country. The Australian officers will work beside the contingent of British officers who will take charge of the training. Gentlemen we will have discipline, obedience and respect for authority. The horses are in excellent condition I cannot say the same for the men."

And so it began.

A daily routine of marching left, right, left, right, left, right. One hundred and ten paces to the minute, trench digging, target practice and all the time immediate and absolute obedience to the officer in command. At least that is what the British Officers hoped for but never fully achieved.

"Hey Murph! Where are you going on Saturday?" Danny O'Dea asked as he threw his backpack next to his bed and tossed his bandoleers next it. The rifles formed a well-arranged teepee in the middle of their exotic tent. It was five pm on Friday 15ᵗʰ of January.

"I think I will go into Cairo and go to the cinema. Some bloke said they are showing a film called 'For the Term of His Natural Life' an Aussie production," Herman replied as he stripped to his waist to have a sponge bath.

'Sounds like us," said Ben Murphy from the back of the tent. "We're here for the term of our natural lives."

"Now I know why Moses led the Jews out of Egypt. Too bloody hot, too bloody sandy and too bloody far away," came the wisdom of Jacky Bunter.

"And bloody Birdie on our backs," chimed in Mick McGuiness.

There were a lot of exotic events to entertain the troops from "Down Under" both in Alexandria and Cairo. The Australian Comfort Committees under the directorship of Mr H.E Budden sprung up everywhere. Apart from a welcoming place for a homesick Aussie to go, they provided billies packed with buttons, shoe laces, chocolate, postcards, soup tablets, insect powder, puzzles, safety pins, bandages, hair brushes, tooth brushes, tooth powder, reading material, tin openers, tinned fish and penknives. There were lots of cafes, which served beer and provided some form of entertainment both on stage and behind closed doors.

"Why don't we take our horses for a ride to the Pyramids?" Richie Burgess suggested as the boys from camp 13 and 14 had a leisurely cup of tea on Saturday morning.

"I would prefer the fleshpots of Cairo. I feel like a woman," said Charlie Bunter.

"You look like one too but I wouldn't go too close to any of the male camels. They might give you a piece of their mind," Mick Siveright joked and copped a dirty wet sock in his face for his trouble.

"Do what you want. I'm going to the cinema," said Herman. "I would keep clear of the women here in Egypt. They will all give you personal diseases."

"I don't think anyone in the 10th has had personal diseases," said Bill Fraser.

"That's because we've got good looking horses, thanks to HJ," joked Les Barndon.

The boys boarded the train for Cairo at the Meadi station. The train left at 9.00 am and by 10.00 am it had reached Bab-al-Louk station. Here they disembarked. Boys and men of all ages noisily requesting the soldiers to hire their vehicle to go to the city approached them.

"My donkey's young, strong,"

"My coach will take you all. No problem."

"My donkey's cheap,"

"My carriage very good, Very good price for strong Aussie soldier."

They settled for two four wheeled carriages each with seating covered in carpets of all colours and state of repair. The owners had obviously thought that the more colours and the more carpets they had in the wagon the more comfortable they would be. The horse that pulled the wagon was not in the best condition but it seemed happy enough. The troopers cringed however when they saw the condition of some of the horses. They had saddle sores and showed signs of being over worked and underfed.

"Let's stop at the Comfort Committees headquarters and see what they've got," said Richie Burgess. He was of course looking for pencils and writing paper and post cards. He kept a journal in which he made an entry each day. He was also a compulsive reader.

"On the way back," was the common cry.

"You'll all be as full as bulls when we come back. I'm getting off," so saying he jumped off.

"I'll come with you," said Tommy Bray." If we don't catch up with you in town, we'll be on the 10.30 train."

Both Tommy and Richie waved as they watched the wagonload of cheering singing soldiers go on their way to the city centre of Cairo. When the soldiers reached their destination they paid the drivers sixpence and walked through the crowded main street of Cairo. The main street was wide and carried all kinds of vehicles from motorbikes to Rolls Royces, from donkeys to camels to horses to single carriages to multiple person carriages. Along the foot paths on each side of the road were people selling beads, freshly made antiques, souvenirs, baskets, carpets, shirts, shawls, native clothing, hats, and fezzes.

"Bloody hell Murph, the only thing they don't sell is their mother," said Bill Fraser after he had said *'no'* to the vendors for the two hundredth time.

"I'm not sure about that. That little fella there wanted to sell me a dress that the lady is wearing. I think he wanted me to buy her as well," Herman replied. He of course was not interested, as he didn't wish to catch syphilis, which was euphemistically a *'personal disease.'* He was also a very good boy.

The streets were so crowded that the lads had to split into groups of two or three. All agreed to meet at Ezbekiya Gardens Café for a drink after they had finished with sightseeing. Herman and Bill wandered the streets and then went to the American Comosgraph Picture Theatre where they watched *'For the Term of His Natural Life.'*

After the show they went to the appointed café. Most of the lads had been there for an hour or so and had enough warm beers to get them in a singing mood. They occupied two tables and had picked up several stray New Zealanders as well. The sweet smell of the shishas combined with the strong smell of Champion Ready Rubbed tobacco, gave the café come cabaret the appearance of the foggy streets of London and the smell of the sewers of Paris. But it was leave time and these were the places you went to let off steam.

The belly dancer danced among the tables.

"Not bad," grinned Jack Bunter.

"You wouldn't know what to do with her if you had her alone," quipped Ben Murphy.

"Yes I would. Give her a bath in Cooper's Dip," replied Bunts.

"Come on lads respect the natives," said Herman. He could not tolerate disrespect to anyone, especially women. When the belly dancer retired, Mick McGuiness grabbed a New Zealander and said. "Come on Kiwi. Let's give them a show." The pair then took to the stage. Jimmy Doherty was a red headed Auckland boy. He was in the New Zealand Artillery. Like Mick he also lacked shyness.

"Good evening folks," Mick began, "As you will note we are not from these parts. I come from Australia and my mate here comes from New Zealand. He speaks a funny sort of English so we forgive you if you don't understand him. We are going to do a little performance for you tonight if the establishment does not mind." Cheers from the crowd made the over large owner of the establishment nod a tentative approval.

"As you know we have a new Commander in Chief. His name is Sir William Birdwood," Mick then began to parade around the stage like the general and then in perfect imitation of the general he began. "It is my duty to mould the New Zealand and the Australian volunteers into a fighting force that will protect the Mother Country. I am duty bound to train them in obedience, discipline and such stupidity that they will follow every order without question. They will always wear a full uniform which includes arms and legs and regulation underwear which they must iron dutifully in the morning and wash dutifully in the evening taking the body out to do so. We will march every day until we drop and then we must crawl and finally slither like a snake until the last drop of sweat has fallen from our brow. Now Sir Private Jimmy Doherty will accompany me in a song. You can all join in. I am sure you know the tune of *The Grand Old Duke of York*. Well here we go:

Grand old Sir William Birdwood,
He had ten thousand men,
He marched them into the desert and then marched them out again
And when they were in, they were in and when they were out they
were out
And when they were half way in they were STUFFED."

Cheers rose from the audience.
"And now I would like to introduce our resident tenor Danny O'Dea."
Danny knew he was going to be called upon so he was waiting stage right.
"Good evening lads. This is a song dedicated to all the Australian and New Zealand volunteers who are holidaying here in Egypt. The Tune follows the Hymn, *'The Church's One Foundation.'* So pay the song a great deal of respect. A New Zealand signaller, Sergeant Keith Little invented the acronym for the Australian and New Zealand volunteers. You here Keith?"

Sergeant Keith Little stood up. He was a rosy checked New Zealander from Christchurch. Cheers rose from the crowd. Sergeant Keith took a humble bow and sat down.

"Good on you Keith. Here we go:

We are the Anzac Army,
The ANZAC.
We cannot shoot, we don't salute,
What the bloody good are we?
And when we get to Ber-lin
The Kaiser he will say
Hoch,hoch! Mein Gott, what a bloody odd lot
To get six bob a day.

Now all together."

The men sang with gusto and cheered and mimicked Sir William.

A shrill whistle suddenly interrupted the revelry. The noise stopped and all turned to the source of the whistle. Standing in front of a curtained private booth was Major Robertson, the aide de camp of General Sir William Birdwood. Then from behind the curtains, Sir William stepped.

All the pins that were dropped could be heard back in Meadi.

"For the record I used the acronym ANZAC well before that colonial signaller. Carry on," said Sir William and walked out the door of the café to his Rolls Royce. He was followed by his aide de camp.

"Hotel D'Ville, major," he commanded the driver.

"No court marshals Sir?" the major asked.

"Not yet," he replied and smiled to himself. He liked the Anzacs. They had spirit.

"Shit Danny I think we will all be shot," said Jack Bunter encouragingly. "Either now or later," Danny responded. "Who's got a drink? I'm thirsty." The new Anzac song resounded through the camp as the men made their way into their tents that night. So the name ANZAC was born and embedded into history.

Chapter 8: First Assault in the Middle East

A strategic network of train lines stretched from Istanbul to Mecca. This meant that in the beginning of the 20th Century one could catch a train in Paris all the way to Mecca except for a slight change of trains and a short walk over the Taurus Mountains in the south of Turkey. With such a network, it was relatively easy to move troops and equipment through the Middle East.

So upon entering the war, Turkey launched a multifronted war with offensives in the Caucasus on the Russian front and in the Sinai on the English front. At the beginning of 1915, a Turkish Army consisting of 20,000 conscripted Anatolian Turks, Armenians, Kurds, Syrians and Arabs accompanied by 11,000 camels marched from the rail head at Gaza across the Sinai desert to cut off the Suez Canal which was a short route to England from her colonies. They dragged steel punts, boats and field guns across the top of the Sinai desert a distance of 150 miles. It took them only fifteen days.

On the 3rd of February 1915 undeterred by aerial strafing from the British Air force, located in Moascar, the Turks attacked the Suez Canal. An Indian Regiment and the 6th Ghurkha rifles from Nepal immediately repelled them. Since a *jihad* had been declared, the Turks were hoping for a rebellion from the Muslims in Egypt. There was no Egyptian rebellion and only twenty-five Turkish soldiers reached the western bank of the Suez and were immediately captured. The Turks withdrew having suffered some 2000 casualties and 700 captives. So the first assault in the Middle East was a victory for the allies. The second assault was of a different nature.

Mick Siveright was very athletic. As a forward pocket he could kick either foot and would bag an average of four goals a match. Sometimes he would exchange to the back pocket. He could drop kick a ball over fifty yards to the mid field. He was however very shrewd. He avoided pain and enjoyed resting. He always had great advice whenever needed. He therefore was a perfect referee for any boxing match. Boxing was a tradition in the armed forces not that Australia had been in existence long enough to establish any form of tradition but it was inherited from the British who had armed forces since the days of old when knights were bold.

A boxing ring had been set up in the recreation tent donated to Meadi camp by the citizens of the suburb. They hoped this would stop the soldiers wandering around their peaceful city. With the Turks' attempt to take the Suez Canal, the citizens began to re think the advantages and disadvantages of having an army camp nearby. Since they could not change this situation, the citizens had decided to be friendly with the troops. The troops did after all provide protection from the enemy.

A crowd of some 200 enthusiasts were seated around the ring.

"Welcome to the opening bout of the art of pugilistic. Following the international code of boxing we have three rounds of three minutes for the Light Heavyweight Championship of camp Meadi. In the red corner we have Les Barndon weighing in at 181 pounds and in the blue corner we have Herman John Murphy weighing in at 185 pounds," Mick Siveright announced in a resounding voice. Then quietly to the two boxers he said, "Go to your corners and come out fighting."

To Herman it was a fun thing to fight. No one got hurt. Just fun. Somehow he had managed to beat every one he had been required to fight in this boxing tournament. Here he was at the grand final and he was fighting his mate but also fighting for the honour of tent 13. Round one was an uneventful round with dancing and weaving. The boxers merely hit each other's gloves. Second round commenced very similar to the first round. Both mates were reluctant to go for a headshot and then Les accidentally hit Herman on the nose. Hell broke loose and Les Barndon was on the canvas within seconds counting little birdies that were twittering overhead. Herman immediately apologized to his mate but all realized that within the big quiet farmer a lion could roar and pack a punch at the same time. Herman also hated being hit on the nose.

During February two more brigades of Australians arrived. One was under the command of Colonel John Monash, an engineer from Melbourne and a full time member of the militia. The other brigade was under the command of Colonel G. Ryrie, a tough pastoralist, politician and one time pugilist. Both of these brigades came under the command of General Sir William Birdwood. By the middle of February the men were using the horses as part of their daily routine drill.

Up the hill, down the hill, dismount, mount, dig trenches and shoot. Up the hill, down the hill from sun up to sun down. The men and the horses began to develop permanent squints because of the sun and sand. At the same time however the horses became acclimatized to the environment and could go long stretches of time and distance without water.

"I think my horse is developing a hump," said Bill Fraser as the men went up another hill during exercises. "It doesn't seem to want to drink as much as it used to."

"Hey Murph! Don't they call this the Promised Land," Jack Bunter asked as he rode beside his cousin.

"I think the Jordan Valley is the Promised Land," replied Herman.

"Well they can have the bloody place as far as I am concerned. It's too hot, too dusty and too bloody far away." When Jack Bunter got an idea, which was not often, he kept on repeating it.

The men were on a four-day march into the desert and back again to get used to the conditions and become hardened soldiers. The drill commenced at sun up and continued through the day until sundown. Usually horses were hobbled when the saddles were removed and the nosebags placed around their necks for the evening meal of oats. The 10th, however, never hobbled their horses. The Aussies trusted their horses to remain close by and they did. Unlike the English, the Aussie trooper had a relationship with the horse. They were mates and the mateship was reciprocated.

"I ain't goin' ta ride a horse no more.
I ain't gonna ride a horse.
My back it aches, my arse is sore.
I ain't gonna ride a horse,"

Tommy Bray sang to himself as he threw his saddle down near the campfire. He would use it as a pillow when he slept under his great coat for the night.

"Billie's boiling," said Herman as he threw two handfuls of tea into the boiling water. He then lifted the billy off the flames with a stick stuck under the handle. Pulling his shirtsleeve down over his hand he picked up the billy and swung it several times around like a windmill and then poured it into the pannikins of his mates who sat exhausted around the fire.

Mick McGuiness pulled out his mouth organ and played an improvised mournful tune. Mick Siveright joined him a little later. Where the tune was going neither knew but it was fun just blowing and sucking. The sound drifted across the cooling desert. A lone fox joined in. The men sat with their thoughts and smoked their last cigarette for the day.

"What are you going to do after the war?" Les Barndon asked Herman Murphy. He held no malice against his mate for knocking him to the canvas.

"Return to the farm. Build a house on the hill near dad's house. Get married and have a few children," Herman replied stoking the fire with a sturdy stick.

"Who will you marry?" Danny O'Dea asked pulling his great coat up to his chin.

"I think he already has his girl picked out. His little flower Iris Reardon," taunted Charlie Bunter.

"Maybe," Herman blushed. "That's enough about me what about the rest of you?"

"We'll all go back to the farm and work our arses off until our kids are old enough to take over," Bill Fraser answered for them all.

"I'm going to get into the business end of things like Charlie," said Mick Siveright.

"I couldn't stand being in an office all day. Farmin' is a good life. It's healthy," said the usually silent Ben Murphy.

"I am going to become a lawyer," said Richie Burgess. "So if any of you get into trouble call on me. I will help you out for a fee."

The evening talk and banter continued until weariness overtook the troopers and they slept soundly

The men returned to camp to receive the Christmas mail and supplies, which had eventually arrived a mere two months late.

Herman took his letter from Iris and sat under the shade of a date palm, a short distance from the camp. He wanted privacy. The handwriting was perfect and large. It had been written with pen and ink.

"Dear Herman

I hope you are well as I am at present. All our family is planning for Christmas. We are going to have a large chook with roast potatoes and pumpkin and a steamed pudding for dessert. I wish you could be here to share it with us.

In the evening we are all going to the Swan River where we will have supper and a swim. I was very sad when I saw you leave on the train to go overseas. I wondered would you ever come back. You can be sure I will be waiting for you.

Your Loving Little Flower,

Iris."

He folded the letter, put it in his pocket and felt very homesick. He went to his tent and under the hurricane lamp, wrote a reply.

"Dear Iris,
Thank you for the letter you sent me. I read it under my favourite date palm tree.
I will return to you so don't worry about that. All the boys here are great fun. We have had several horse races. I entered Peter in one of them but I think I am too heavy to be a jockey. We had a sports meeting against the other camps. We won easily. Charlie Bunter won the hundred yards, I won the high jump and Tommy Bray won the mile. There are lots of interesting sites here in Egypt. We have ridden out to the Pyramids and been through the Cairo museum. It is very hot in this country and is starting to get hotter. I don't think we will do any fighting. We just do a lot of drilling so there is no need to worry about me not returning.
Lots of Love,
Herman."

He slept thinking of his home and his future.
Saturday morning. Richie Burgess was reading a late issue of the Egyptian Gazette.
"Listen to this," said Richie burgess." I think we are winning the war." The members of camp 14 and 13 continued polishing their leathers-boots, saddle, strapping-as Richie read out the choice piece of news.

"The Prime Minister of Britain H, H Asquith dismissively mocked the Turks invasion of the Suez Canal on the 3rd of February when he said in a letter to this press: 'The Turks have been trying to throw

a bridge across the Suez Canal and in that ingenious way find a way into Egypt. The poor things and their 'would be bridge' were blown to smithereens and they have retired to the other side of the desert.'"

"Is there a war on?" asked Danny O'Dea jokingly. "I thought we were here to march in and out of the desert."

As the Anzacs were being formed into a fighting unit and were being marched into the desert and out again, the heads of Britain were devising methods to win the war and make their territorial gains as quickly as possible.

"If we strike the Turk at Constantinople and take the capital, the Ottoman Empire will fall. Russia is on our side so the Germans are hemmed in at the East. We would be able to strengthen the western front and the war would be over by August or Christmas at the latest," said Winston Churchill, Head of the Admiralty.

A single plan sounded so plausible in the leathered political room of Britain. The plan was put into motion. But before it really began celebrations were called for by the troops in Egypt. On the 2nd of April, Good Friday, almost the whole Meadi, Mena and Zeitoun camps converged on Cairo to celebrate with their comrades in arms. The Infantry and Artillery Brigades from both Mena and Zeitoun were to move out on the 9th of April for a destination unknown yet everyone knew it was Gallipoli.

They sang their way to Bab al-Louk Station. Here each hired a donkey and raced to the Wasser Café, a frequented grog and girl café in down town Cairo. They burst into the café singing

We are the Anzac army
The ANZAC.
We cannot shoot, we don't salute,

What the bloody good are we?
And when we get to Ber lin
The Kaiser he will say
Hoch, hoch! Mein Gott, what a bloody odd lot
To get six bob a day.

They occupied three tables and sang and drank and laughed their way through the afternoon. They mixed readily with the infantry and artillery.

"If you blokes from the infantry and artillery get into trouble, just call in the cavalry," Bill Fraser remarked to a few of the boys from Camp Mena.

"Look mate when Johnny Turk cops a view of us, he will run all the way to China. We'll be back in a couple of days," Private Merv MacIntosh from the 2nd Infantry Brigade responded light heartedly. Their revelry stopped when from near the front of the café, a table was over turned and a chair smashed to the floor. The waiter, considering the soldiers to be a little too intoxicated had increased the drink bill to a total that almost gave him a round trip to France.

"Get out of here you bloody wog. I am not paying that bill. No way is that right. You bloody cheat." Gunner Monterolo said angrily.

"You bastards piss me off." He then hit the rotund waiter a resounding blow to the chin with his fist. The waiter was thrown backwards knocking over tables and glasses.

"Not one of us," said Jack Bunter holding onto his beer and looking to see who caused the raucous.

"Some bloke from the infantry. It looks like a bloody pommy," said Les Barndon picking his glass up and moving to the door of the cafe.

Then it was on for young and old. Bottles, glasses, fists, mud, slush and beer everywhere. The riot continued out on the street. Mattresses came flying from nearby brothels. Police, with batons, natives with knives, women screaming, all mixed in the farewell party for the Anzacs.

"Looks like the floor show has finished," said Herman Murphy and stood up and walked into the fresh air. He was followed by the men of tent 13 and 14. They quietly walked to the railway station. Boarded the 10.30 pm train and were all in bed by midnight. The riot at Wasser had resulted in three deaths, several houses were burnt down and many prostitutes were without mattresses for some time. The records show that the members of the 10th were innocent as usual. Really!

The 10th Light Horse formed a Guard of Honour for the Anzacs heading for Gallipoli on the 9th of April. They lined the exit of both Mena camps and Zeitoun camp. The Anzacs marched out of the camps proudly. Each man carried his own kit bag and rifle. *"Good luck mate," "Take care cobber,"* were expressions that could be heard all along the line.

The troops boarded the trains, which took them the 154 miles to Port Said. Here they embarked on ships that took them across the Mediterranean Sea. The journey was about ten days. The ships gathered in Mudros Harbour on Limnos Island, which was 80 miles from Gallipoli.

Chapter 9: Gallipoli

The British War Office loved names that would sound good in their respective memoirs. The troops invading Gallipoli were initially called the Constantinople Expeditionary Force. A very nice name indeed!

The invasion was the worst kept secret in history. Everyone knew where the troops from Egypt were going. Even the price of wheat in Chicago dropped because everyone thought there would be no difficulty for Russia bringing their wheat crop through the liberated straits of the Bosphorus and the Dardanelles. In February and March, the British artillery bombarded the Gallipoli Peninsula from the sea, to soften up the enemy for the proposed landing. The infantry and artillery battalions were the first to depart for Gallipoli. The whole campaign was designed and implemented in haste.

Lord Kitchener, the Secretary of State for War selected his chief of staff, the 62 year old, Sir Ian Hamilton to be the Commander in Chief of the operation. Sir Ian Hamilton had shown promise in his youth but the clanship and sycophancy of the British Officer Class saw him giving into his seniors. Hamilton failed to impose his own rules on his generals.

The maps and medical facilities were inadequate. The information about the terrain and the strength of the resistance was inadequate. Up to date knowledge gained from aerial reconnaissance about tents, trenches and gun batteries were inadequate. So the commander of the Gallipoli Campaign could very well be called Captain Inadequate. Rupert Brooke, the handsomest man in England, who after a tour of duty in Belgium wrote poems about the war, was the first casualty in the Gallipoli campaign. He died from a mosquito bite on the lip. It became septic and he died. On The 23rd of April twelve Australian soldiers took his coffin to an olive grove in Skyros, an island some 80 miles south of Limnos. The following poem struck a harmonious cord with many of the family members who had a member of their family at war.

The Soldier

If I should die, think only this of me:
    That there's some corner of a foreign field
That is for ever England. There shall be
    In that rich earth a richer dust concealed;
A dust whom England bore, shaped, made aware,
    Gave, once, her flowers to love, her ways to roam,
A body of England's, breathing English air,
    Washed by the rivers, blest by suns of home.
And think, this heart, all evil shed away,
    A pulse in the eternal mind, no less
Gives somewhere back the thoughts by England given;
Her sights and sounds; dreams happy as her day;
    And laughter, learnt of friends; and gentleness,
In hearts at peace, under an English heaven.
Rupert Brooke (1887-1915)

The first ship slipped from Mudros Harbour and one of the mightiest seaborne invasions in history was about to commence. It was the first of 200 ships. The soldiers and sailors of the other ships cheered. The sky was cloudless and the spring flowers of the Greek Island danced a merry goodbye. Although there was both a French and British Division in the invasion force, the Australians were to be the first troops going ashore. Their objective was to land at Gallipoli and make their way along the 132 miles to capture Constantinople, the capital of Turkey and the Islamic world.

"Breakfast at Gallipoli, Lunch at Tekirdag and dinner at Constantinople," was Winston Churchill's boast.

The Gallipoli Peninsula guarded the three seas of antiquity, the Sea of Marmara, the Mediterranean Sea and the Black Sea. On the other side of the Dardanelles was the ancient city of Troy, now a mere ruin. Several miles from Troy was the town of Canakkale. Here the British navy had been defeated in March 1915. So a land invasion at Gallipoli was decided as plan B. This was a brilliant strategy. The mastermind behind it was Winston Churchill an aspiring politician at the age of 41. He was the First Lord of the Admiralty. Nothing was spared for this invasion.

It is ironic that most of the munitions used by the Turks had been made by Vickers, a British Company. They had been made while Turkey was an ally of Britain.

At the outbreak of the war Turkey still had battleships being built in the British ship building yards. The British impounded them in August 1914. The money for these vessels had been collected from the ordinary villagers throughout Turkey. In anger the Turks had turned to Germany for assistance, which was readily given.

Time and time again the city of Troy had been invaded. This time the invasion was on the other side of the strait. Turkey was never very happy about being invaded. The history of Troy shows that the Turks did not welcome invaders.

The decks of the moving ships from Mudros were overcrowded with raw Anzac troops who had never seen battle before. The voices of over ten thousand voices were raised in song. They sang:

> *'Australia Will Be There:*
> *On land or sea, wherever you may be*
> *Keep your eye on Germany!*
> *For England Home and Beauty*
> *Have no cause to fear!*
> *Should auld acquaintance be forgot?*
> *No! No! No! No! No! Australia will be there!*
> *Australia will be there!'*

With the exhilarating feeling of waiting to run onto a football field at a grand final, the troops sat quietly on the ships decks. At 1.00 am on the 25th of April 1915, the ships halted. The boys climbed down the rope ladders into the rowing boats. At 3.30 am steamboats towed them ashore. Moving in darkness the boats glided onto the seashore pebbles about a mile north of Gaba Tepe, at a place called Ariburnu, the Bay of Bees, so named because of all the wild bumblebees that inhabited the pitted cliff face. It was soon to be known as Anzac Cove.

As dawn broke the troops waded ashore. The Turks watched. Ahmed Rashid sat in a trench overlooking the Bay of Bees. He with his companions made up the 160 men who guarded this section of the Gallipoli Peninsula.

"Shit! Look at this," Ahmed gasped and nudged his mate who was asleep.

The leaders of the Constantinople Expeditionary Force had no knowledge of the land. They did not know where the high ground was. They had no accurate maps. They had no courage to make a decision other than not listen to any Australians. The British Officers considered the Australians to be ignorant by nature. In addition to the lack of knowledge of the terrain, communication was ineffective so the men were left to their own devices. Some worked their way up to the upper ridges and caught glimpses of the Narrows. The Narrows is a mile wide stretch of water. Next stop should have been Constantinople but the Australian troops had to turn back or be killed for close in the hinterland riding in front of his Division of 12,000 men was Mustafa Kemal.

The overall commander of the Turkish troops was Liman von Sander a 64 year old, resolute, stout German General. He had been sent to Turkey a year earlier to reorganize the Ottoman Army. Apart from being a fastidious dresser and cavalry officer, he had little in common with Kemal. Mustafa Kemal was thirty-four. He had steely blue eyes, brown hair and was filled with charisma, energy and love for his country. He was a well-educated son of a customs clerk. He could speak French fluently. He had polished manners and an eye catching dignified deportment that made him a welcome guest at many a Grand Ball. But above all, his men would follow him anywhere. They gave him ultimate loyalty and trust. He was later called the Saviour of Gallipoli.

Like the coach of a football team, he kept shifting his men here and there to positions where they would be most effective. As the Australians reached the top of the ridge, Kemal shifted his gun batteries to break up the onslaught. He pushed battalions forward to break up the troops clawing their way up the cliffs. He moved howitzers forward to bombard the boats continually bringing troops ashore. Half of the Anzacs who landed on the first couple of days were casualties.

> *From the 25th to 28th of April the score was:*
> *Killed: 2,500 men and 150 officers.*
> *Wounded: 6,000 men and 250 officers.*

The first objective of the Australians was to capture the third ridge of the Sari Bair Range. This was the stepping-stone to the Narrows, commonly called the Dardinelles. Kemal knew that whoever commanded the heights controlled the entire area. So he immediately seized high ground. The Turks fought with such ferocity that the Australians were driven back. They dug into the coastal spurs and ridges. The Anzacs had very little protection and no support from the ships at sea. The ships could deliver supplies and new troops but because the Turks and the Anzacs were so close to each other and their uniforms were the same colour, the ships were fearful of hitting their own men. Confusion, therefore, ruled supreme.

There was difficulty in getting the wounded from the trenches and the beaches onto transports. Many of the vessels moving the wounded were neither staffed nor equipped to take them on board. For example on the *Hindoo* there were two medical officers and two surgical panniers to care for 800 casualties. On the *SS Lutzow* one lone veterinary surgeon was expected to care for 600 wounded during the four-day voyage to back to Egypt. The reporting of the casualties was covered up. By the time the Australians back home read of 50 casualties there were 5,000 at least. John Masefield, the poet laureate for England, horrified by the inadequate support, raised a small flotilla, which he brought from England, through the Mediterranean to Gallipoli. Each night he would collect the British, French and Anzacs wounded from the beaches.

By the end of May over 17,000 wounded had to be housed somewhere in Egypt. Norman Brookes, Australia's champion tennis player who won Wimbledon in 1914, headed the Red Cross in Cairo. A temporary hospital was set up in Luna Park in Heliopolis. Mudros, the island some eighty miles from Gallipoli, took 6,000. Another hospital was set up at Atelier, a suburb of Cairo. Here a tarpaulin was thrown over the tennis courts at the Ghezireh Sporting club. Two Australian hospitals were established at Lemnos, an Island off the coast of Gallipoli. To add to the shortage of hospitals and carers the men had been separated from their kits so had no clothes or toiletries. It was a mess. The men of the 10th were called upon to help.

"You men have to go into Cairo to give assistance to the soldiers returning from Gallipoli," Major Maloney directed his squadron at parade on the 30th of April.
"They all coming back or just a few?" asked Herman.

"Bugger me. They said they would get it done in a couple of days. I didn't really believe them," chimed in Jack Bunter, thinking that Constantinople had been taken.

"The war will be over before I fire a shot," said Bill McGuiness.

"Things haven't gone too well," added Major Maloney. "These are the wounded. We have to help. The battle is still going on."

The men waited at Bab al Louk station. They were not sure what to expect but what arrived was beyond their wildest dreams. Troop trains were usually a rowdy affair, with soldiers hanging out of windows shouting, whistling and singing. The train pulled into the station was like a ghost train. The only sound was that made by the engine and clickity clack of steel on steel. The train moaned to a stop. There was silence.

"Where are they?" asked Jack Bunter. "The bloody train's empty."

The train then disgorged its contents.

Assisted by Red Cross, female and male nurses, men with blackened faces and blood stained shirts and trousers disembarked. The 10th immediately went into action. They put the men into lorries and commandeered every movable machine, man or beast and began to move the wounded.

"Where to?" Bill Fraser asked.

"To the Gezireh Club. We can use the tennis courts there," Norman Brookes replied.

"Here digger. Have a smoke," Herman passed a rolly to a soldier who had a piece of dirty blackened blood stained cloth, that looked like underwear, wrapped around his head and covering one eye.

"Ta," the infantryman replied and took one drag and then coughed up blood.

"Rough?" Herman asked.

"Yep," was the reply and then he died.

The advantage of the soldiers dying was that it made space for the wounded who were living. The entourage of dead and dying and wounded reached the Gezireh Club.

The wounded were laid in rows and the nurses moved among the men giving them water and encouragement. The dead were put to the side to await transport to a burial ground that had not yet been organized.

"Come on lads! These lads can't lie in the sun. We need to get some sort of covering," Herman said and together he and his mates did a tour of the town with their horse drawn lorries. They returned with carpets, cushions, canvases, and woollen tents. Together they built the tennis court hospital.

"Birdie wants you blokes back at the camp by sunset," said Lieutenant Forester a signaller working for General Sir William Birdwood.

"Tell him to get stuffed. We're look'n after our mates," said Jack Bunter as he fixed a black and white Bedouin woollen tent to the wire wall of the tennis courts.

"I beg your pardon?" replied the British officer rising to his full five foot six inches.

"Don't worry Sir," said Richie Burgess in quiet mellowed tones and he stood to his full six foot three inches. "We'll be there. We are a bit upset that our mates are not getting medical attention. Fifteen have died since we brought them in."

"So tell the little fat arse *pommy* to get here and help," added Jack Bunter who always had a way with words.

Fortunately the English lieutenant did not quite understand the Australian patois but impressed by Richie's aristocratic bearing, he left.

"Bloody pommy bastard," said Bunts and jumped down from his woollen wall.

The men returned to camp by sunrise, next morning. They had a cup of tea and reported to the parade grounds. Birdie was immaculate. The men were unshaven, dishevelled and didn't give a *"rat's arse."* He addressed the men

"The combined British, French and Anzac forces apparently require reinforcements. We therefore call upon the Light Horse to assist in the operation at Gallipoli. You will go as infantry and we will only take volunteers. Each commanding officer will select several men from each squad to remain behind to care for the horses. The volunteers need to be ready to move out as soon as possible. Volunteers need to report to your squadron leaders."

The Light Horse volunteered to a man.

"Sorry Murph," apologised Major Maloney. "You know the horses better than anyone. So I have to ask you to stay behind. You will be given temporary promotion to the position of sergeant. There will be no extra pay but you will be in charge of all the lads remaining behind."

"How many is that?" Herman asked not at all thrilled with being separated from his mates.

"Fifty men and 500 horses all together,"

"Right," Herman responded and his mind began to immediately work out a schedule to ensure the horses would be in top condition when his mates returned.

The men's last day in camp was Saturday the 15th of May. No leave had been granted. The men had to use the time to ensure their kit was ready for the oncoming battle.

"What do you reckon it is like?" Mick McGuiness asked as the men sat around their campfire having a cup of billy tea laced with rum. The last light of the sun decorated the sky with gold.

"They reckon you stand on the beach and let Johnny Turk take pot shots at ya," said Bill McGuiness as tobacco spilt out of his Ritz cigarette paper and he had to roll his cigarette again.

"One of the guys said that the Aussies are diggin' into the cliff that is next to the beach," said Ben Murphy as he shifted his feet a little closer to the fire.

"How far are they from Constantinople anyway?" asked Charlie Bunter.

"Up the cliff over the ridge and then a four mile hike and you will have all the Turkish delight you can find," said Mick Siveright.

"More like a hundred and ninety-four," corrected Richie Burgess who was taking notes by the campfire light.

"Once you start running, they won't stop you Mick," said Les Barndon who was on his third cup of rum with a little tea.

"I believe they have a lot of books in Constantinople, Richie. You'll be able to catch up on your reading," said Tommy Bray, his cross-fingered hands behind his head looked at the stars that had started to appear.

"They have a few," Richie agreed and looked pensively into the fire.

"Well I hope we don't have to do any bayonet charging. What is it again? Hit under chin, shove your bayonet in, put your foot on 'em and pull it out?" asked Jack Bunter.

"Don't worry Bunts if you can't remember, Johnny Turk will show you how," said Bill Fraser.

"Not on my shirt he won't. I just ironed it," replied the blonde trooper.

"We'll miss you Murph. But make sure our horses are in top condition when we return," encouraged Danny O'Dea knowing the big farmer was sad because he was not going with his mates.

"They'll be in top condition, don't you worry. Anyway you'll all be back in a couple of days," Herman responded and his mind shifted to the sight of the ghost train that brought the injured from Gallipoli a few days earlier.

The men talked until midnight and one by one drifted off to their tents where they slept fitfully.

They were up well before reveille and had their tea, followed by a hearty breakfast.

The seven o'clock train was idling expectantly as the men marched through the main street of Maadi to greet it. Herman had his troop form a guard of honour for the 2,250 men and 106 officers from the 2nd and 10th Light Horse who boarded the train.

The lads from tent 13 and 14 stopped when they reached the door of their carriage, turned and saluted their mates who were left behind.

Big Bill Fraser black hair, cleft chin and turned up nose. Always serious.

Tommy Bray with his hat sitting on the back of his head and his curly hair sticking out in front. He had a cheeky grin that was permanent.

Richie Burgess tall, thoughtful, pointed features. He flashed a rare smile at Herman.

Les Barndon strong and stocky, blue eyes flashed with excitement.

Mick Siveright eyes darting every which way looking for a deal.

Danny O'Dea tall. The great songster whose eyes disappeared when he laughed which he did often.

Ben Murphy sober and solid, always there to help.

Mick McGuiness handsome, cheeky, athletic.

Bill McGuiness chubby cheeks and contagious laugh.

Charlie Bunter handsome, the ladies' man.

Jack Bunter with his quizzical look, his spikey, blonde hair and his smart quip.

They were all swallowed up by the train. It moved off and with it the sounds of the voices of the men as they sang, *'Pack up Your Troubles in Your Old Kit Bag.'*

The guard of honour dispersed as the train puffed away and immediately went into action of exercising and grooming the horses. Routine was the salve to Herman's pain caused by the departure of his mates.

Chapter 10: The Tenth Will Be There

The Second and Tenth Regiments of the Australian Light Horse boarded a German Steamer at Suez. It had been commandeered by the British.

"This is a bloody rust bucket," said Jack Bunter as he sat on the deck next to Danny O'Dea.

"I think the cleaners must be permanently out to lunch," replied Danny.

"I'm sitting in lunch," said Bill McGuiness as he kicked some food scraps off the deck into the sea.

The men had their sleeping quarters either on deck or in the long 'holds' of the 'once upon a time' freighter. The air was thick, as summer had started to warm the Northern Hemisphere. Toilets were non-existent except for the long drop to the ocean from the 'poop' deck. Grindstones were available for the soldiers to entertain themselves by sharpening their bayonets. The men slept and woke and woke and slept.

"Right men it's time to go," Major Maloney said as he walked along the decks. "Good luck."

"Now it's, hit under chin, shove it in, foot on chest, pull it out," said Bunts to Danny O'Dea.

"Quiet lads," whispered Bill Fraser as they slipped over the side of the ship and climbed down the loose rope ladders into the waiting barges.

"This is something we never practised," said Tommy Bray.

They packed into the front of the barge.

"Don't jump over the side until we hit the sand," said Bill Fraser.
He received acknowledgement through a series of grunts.

"When we hit the beach, we make our way to the left and dig in. The place is called Plugges Plateau," explained Bill Fraser.

"How do you spell that?" asked Bill McGuiness nervously.

"I went to a beach once," joked Mick Siveright. "Very much like this. It had water and sand."

"I think Johnny Turk is preparing a welcome for us," said Bill Fraser as Kemal's howitzers began to deter any one from landing on the beach. Shrapnel and pebbles chinked the side of the barge as its bow dug into the beach and was followed by a spray of machine gun bullets.

"Wait for it!" Bill ordered his mates as he waited for the slightest break in the gunfire from the ridge overlooking the beach. "Now!" he called and men scrambled over the sides of the barge and followed their acknowledged leader, Bill Fraser, to Plugges Plateau. Shallow trenches had already been dug. The men jumped in.

"They don't let up do they," said Jack Bunter as he curled into the smallest ball possible.

"Oh bugger," said Mick Siveright. He stood up and fired several rounds into the ridge where the machine gun foxhole was positioned.

"Get down soldier," an authoritative voice called.

"I can't sit here and let them take pot shots at me," responded Mick disrespectfully and under his breath he said. "Bloody idiot! I bet he's one of those *pommy bastards.*"

They stayed in the trenches for forty-eight hours and then made their way to a small gully christened Monash Gully.

"Chauvel is our leader," said Richie Burgess. "Harry Chauvel. He's a toffy Queenslander."

"As long as he is an Aussie," replied Bill McGuiness.

On the 24th of May an armistice was declared so both the Turks and Anzacs could remove the dead and wounded from No Man's Land. The 10th assisted with the removal of the wounded.

On the morning of the 29th at 3.20 am the Turks began battering the trenches at Quinn's Post. The 10th returned fire. Soon their ammunition began to run low.

"Bugger this," said Bill Fraser. He fixed his bayonet turned to his mates and said. "Who's comin?" He cleared the sandbags on the top of the trenches and took off. About a hundred Aussies followed him.

Bunts was repeating to himself, "Hit 'em under the chin, shove your bayonet in, put your foot on 'em, pull it out."

It was a surprise to the Turks because it was so foolhardy. The Aussies were in the foxholes and trenches before the Turks realized it.

Jack Bunter jumped a pile of sand bags. He landed three feet from two Turks. He fired a round into one. The bullet struck the young Turk in the head killing him instantly. The other Turk reached for his rifle but Bunts was too quick. He swung his rifle and hit the unsuspecting Turk under the chin. The stunned Turk fell to his knees; Jack pushed the thirty-five inch bayonet into the Turk's body just below his sternum. The blade cut his heart in half. He looked into Bunts's eyes as his life poured out. "Put your foot on 'em and pull it out." Jack Bunter's adrenaline was pumping faster than his blood. He leapt into another foxhole and repeated the exercise. But then the next trenches were empty.

"Looks like they've taken a hike," said Tommy Bray as he slid down the side of a Turkish trench, cocked his hat on the back of his head and rolled himself a smoke.

"It sounds as if those men of the 10th live up to their motto, '*Strike and Strike Swiftly*'," said Harry Chauval proudly. "But they must learn discipline. We must be coordinated if we wish to win this war."

July was the middle of summer in Gallipoli. Temperatures reached 110 degrees Fahrenheit. The surrounding land stank of decomposing bodies of the dead soldiers. Large blue bottle flies flew from the bodies to the food the Aussies ate. The '*Turkey Trot*' as diarrhoea was jokingly called, began its merry dance. Of the 43,553 wounded and sick taken from Gallipoli 12,968 were suffering from dysentery.

On the 6th of August about two and half miles north of Anzac Cove, 30,000 men from the New Army and Territorial Divisions landed at Suvla Bay, They took the Turks by surprise. Quickly the New Army moved onto the plateau. Sir Frederick Stopford was in charge. He continued to use delaying tactics where speed was required. Kemal was soon able to fill the gaps and force the New Army back. Sir Frederick Stopford lived up to his name. He was more stop than go. So delays and hesitation cost the advantage of surprise with the Suvla landing.

Of the 50,000 British and Anzac troops who landed at Suvla Bay, 2,000 were killed and over 22,000 sick and wounded were returned to Egypt and Malta. Impatience to break out of Anzac Cove greeted this failed attack. This led to the assault on Nek a few weeks later. Nek was a narrow rocky ridge fifty yards wide and twenty yards long. The Aussies were at one end. The Turks were at the other. It was like charging from the end of one basketball court to the other. "If we can break through at Nek, we can move all the way to Constantinople with little or no opposition," was the naive thinking of the leadership. The simple plan had not been discussed with the Turks who had devised a counter plan to shoot anyone who tried to cross the small ridge.

The 10th were to do this simple task. The charge was to commence in the early hours of dawn. It was thought that the half-light of dawn would provide sufficient cover. The Turkish trenches were to be bombarded from the ships at sea before the charge commenced. At 4.00 am the bombardment started. The target was missed completely. The bombardment ceased at 4.23 am, some seven minutes before the Anzacs were to charge giving the Turks plenty of time to prepare for the charge.

"Lines of 150, men," was the order.

In the front row was Bill Fraser, on his right stood Danny O'Dea, Mick McGuiness, and Ben Murphy, on his left was Bill McGuiness and Charlie Bunter.

"I'm right behind you Bill," said Jack Bunter. Bunts was in the second row and on his right were Richie Burgess and Les Barndon, on his left were Mick Siveright and Tommy Bray.

The shelling deafened the men as they stood in their orderly rows.

"This'll be the fastest sprint you've ever run, Charlie," Bill McGuiness said to his cousin.

"Piece of cake," said Charlie.

"Just another Grand Final lads," shouted Bill Fraser over the canon fire.

"How many bloody Grand Finals do we have to play?" returned Mick McGuiness.

The shelling stopped. Silence filled the air. The Aussies heard the machine guns of the Turks being cocked. The only other sound was the murmur of Jack Bunter. "Hit 'em under the chin. Shove your bayonet in. Put your foot on them. Pull it out"

The whistle blew.

The men sprang into action. Charlie Bunter was the first to hit the top of the trench. His legs were shot from under him and fell back into the trench. He had not taken a step. Bill Fraser made two yards. The machine gun bullets peppered his chest killing him instantly. Danny covered three yards and dropped. Successive machine gun bullets had opened his stomach. Mick McGuiness's handsome face disappeared as the bullets shredded it. Both Ben Murphy and Bill McGuiness were the slowest of the group but they got the furthest. They both covered five yards and fell dead. A single bullet went straight through Ben's heart and a single bullet went thrown Bill Mac's brain.

"Next group! Step up!" the Officer called.

"Hit 'em under the chin . . ."

The whistle blew. Bunts jumped and a bullet went straight through his head. He was dead.

Richie Burgess was dead at the fifth yard, Les Barndon on the sixth. Mick Siveright and Tommy Bray fell together at the eighth.

"Next line up!"

Whistle

"Charge!"

All dead.

"Next line up."

The order was countermanded. "Stand down lads."

Five hundred men charged that morning. Three hundred died.

"Shit, your legs coped a bashing," said the medic as he lifted Charlie Bunter onto the stretched.

"Yeah! I stepped into a rabbit trap," he replied but he could not feel anything. His mind was occupied with the images of his mates all laughing at him as they ran out on the football field of his mind.

Ten days later he was off loaded at Cairo. Herman was there.

"Where are the rest?" he asked.

"All gone mate," replied Charlie.

Suddenly the big adventure had become serious. An emotion he had never felt before pervaded Herman's whole body like a branding iron on his soul. He assisted his cousin and found him a place to rest in the tennis court hospital. Charlie was placed in line to wait for surgery. The legs which could once dance all night and run at a speed of 10 seconds to the hundred yards were removed and buried.

"I always wanted to donate something to Egypt," he joked as he was assisted onto the boat for home.

"See ya Murph. I might get a job driving a lift. What do you think?" asked Charlie.

"A great idea," replied Herman. Charlie boarded a ship that had delivered another division of ignorant, young colonials to take the place of those who had been killed.

Gallipoli was a cover up. A cover up of the number of casualties. A cover up of the incompetence of the British command, beginning with Sir Ian Hamilton at the top to the officer at the bottom. A cover up of the bungled delivery of supplies and ammunition. A cover up of an invasion of another country for the purpose of extending the British Empire into the Middle East and the acquisition of land and property. Keith Murdoch, a young Melbourne journalist, endeavoured to reveal the truth.

He got permission to visit Gallipoli. He was on route to England to take up a position with the cable news. He was appalled with the conditions under which the soldiers were expected to exist. The official British journalist, Ellis Ashmead Bartlett, echoed his thoughts. Murdoch smuggled a letter out of Imbros, the second base of the British for Gallipoli, from Ellis Ashmead Bartlett to the Prime Minister Asquith. A British intelligence officer confiscated the letters when Murdoch's ship docked at Marseilles. Undaunted Murdoch wrote to the Prime Minister of Australia. A copy of the letter was sent to Lloyd George the Minister for Munitions in Britain. Lloyd George passed it onto the Prime Minister of England. As a consequence of this letter, Sir Ian Hamilton was sacked and given no further position. Lieutenant General Sir William Birdwood took temporary command of operations until Sir Charles Monroe, the new commander, took up the position.

The winter came. It was as ruthless as the summer. Incessant rains turned trenches into ponds of mud. Then came the cold and many soldiers froze to death. In November Kitchener made a visit to the front lines. He immediately decided on withdrawal. On December 8th 1915, Kitchener sent the order to Gallipoli Headquarters. *"Cabinet has decided to evacuate positions at Suvla and Anzac at once"*.
"Wars are not won by retreats," objected Winston Churchill who took another sip from his whiskey glass in the warm rooms of the Admiralty.

Later in that cold December the departure of the troops from Gallipoli was carried out without loss of life. Kemal on the ridges of Gallipoli watched the withdrawal of troops from Gallipoli. He had ordered token opposition. *"Let them pass,"* he said. *"I have never seen so many lions led by so many lambs."*

During eight months of fighting, 43,000 Allied troops had been killed or had died of disease. Of the 410,000 British troops and 79,000 French troops sent to Gallipoli the casualties were:

British: 205,000 casualties including 28,000 Australians

(115,000 killed wounded or missing, 90,000 evacuated sick)

French casualties: 47,000.

Turkish casualties: 251,000.

Captain Clementine Atlee was the last to leave. On December 19th at 5.00 pm he led 205 men to the beach and boarded the *HMS Princess Irene*. Atlee looked back at what had been one of the greatest fiascos in war history. He later became the Prime Minister of England. Mustafa Kemal watched from the ridges on his brilliant white horse. He later became the Head of the New Turkey and was called Kemal Ataturk-the Father of Turkey.

Yet another Troy had sent its invaders packing.

Chapter 11: Australia Pays

The official eighteen million pounds that Australia borrowed from England to equip the first Australian Imperial Forces (AIF) had increased rapidly each week. Every bullet, every boot and every crumb of food put Australia further in debt. When the amount reached fifty million pounds, the Bank of England declined further loans and the money had to be raised in Australia. The debt was increased further because of charges made by the British Government for quartering the AIF in France and providing provisions.

Such was the patriotism in Australia that not only were the loan monies raised but also the number of troops recruited increased. True evidence of Aussie children caring for Mother England!

Chapter 12: Arab Nationalism

On the 20th of August 1915 after the landing at Suvla Bay, a twenty eight year old Turkish Officer, Muhammad Sharif al Faruqi crossed *'no man's land'* waving a white flag. He stated he was a deserter. He was submitted to continuous interrogation but at the same time enjoying accommodation in the best hotel in Egypt. He gave information about the Turkish positions and strengths and leaders. He also spoke of the rise of Arabic nationalism. He contended that the Arabs were ready to rise up and throw off the yoke of the Ottoman Empire. He spoke of secret societies and underground resistance. All of this information was fiction.

There was no cohesion among the Arab tribes and there was no thought of Arab Nations. The British however believed it was so. The renowned Lawrence of Arabia believed it was so. They believed there was a ground swell of Arab nationalism and the Arabs were ready to rebel against the Ottoman Empire. Under the Ottoman Empire, the Sultans of Constantinople for three centuries were both rulers and religious leaders of the Empire. The Cloak of the Holy Prophet Mohammed was held in Constantinople. The Sultans of Constantinople controlled the Holy cities of Medina and Mecca. Without these cities, it would be difficult for them to be the titular leaders of the Sunni Muslims.

The Sultan's standing was dependent on the ruler of the Hejaz Sector, in which were the cities of Medina and Mecca. The ruler of the Hejaz sector was Sherif Hussein. He was also the head of the Hashemite clan in the Hejaz sector. Large garrisons of Turkish troops were kept in Hejaz to ensure that Sherif Hussein remained subservient to Constantinople and did not turn his emirate into an independent principality. Britain on the other hand wanted Sherif Hussein to be free of Constantinople and rule the cities of Mecca and Medina. This would give the Muslims of the British Empire free access to these holy places. Hussien however had ambitions of his own. He wanted to be king of a great Arab nation with his sons Ali, Abdullah, Feisal and Zeid as rulers of Confederate Arab States.

Moved by Faruqi's information and Lawrence's fantasy, the British politicians saw the opportunity of another strategy to undermine the Ottoman Empire and organize the Middle East to their advantage. Arthur MacMahon, the British High Commissioner sent a letter to Hussein promising support for Hussein to become independent in Hejaz. It was not quite what Hussein wanted. He wanted an assurance that on the conclusion of the war all Arab lands under Ottoman control would be given self-rule. A letter written on the 24th October known as the *'Hussein-MacMahon Correspondence'* agreed to Hussein's demands. Hussein was to instigate the Arab revolt but he lacked arms, money, a strong army and food. He also lacked administrative ability and failed to keep the Bedouins from robbing and exploiting pilgrims.

Coinciding with the *'Hussein-MacMahon Agreement'* was the *'Sykes-Picot Agreement'*. This was an agreement between the French and the English. In this agreement England and France had divided up the territories of the Ottoman Empire between themselves. It consisted of a map of the Turkish provinces on which some were marked with red for the English and those marked with blue were for France while those marked in brown were for Palestine. The brown areas were sacred to Muslims, Jews and Christians. The owner of this territory was to be determined by a meeting to be held later with Russia, France and Great Britain.

While the *'leather chaired set'* was playing *'this for that'* in plush hotel rooms, the demoralised Aussie troops arrived back from a failed Gallipoli campaign.

Chapter 13: Back in the Saddle Again

A depleted 10th Light Horse marched into Camp Meadi on the 23rd of December. Christmas was a very sombre affair. The first scars of war were ever present. There was no Danny O'Dea to lead the carol singing nor Jack Bunter to make wisecracks. The quiet wisdom of Richie Burgess was absent. Tommy Bray's incessant giggling could not be heard. The bumbling leadership of Bill Fraser was not there. Smiling faces and raucous laughter over simple things were absent that Christmas. Herman returned to empty tents after the midnight service.

The depleted regiments were brought up to strength with new recruits.

On the 5th of January 1916 Herman was in his tent writing to Iris.

"G'day mate." Herman looked up and there at the entrance to the tent was a smiling face.

"Paul Flanagan's my name. Are you Herman Murphy?"

"Yes mate," Herman acknowledged the new comer. "What can I do for you?"

"I'm a replacement. Major Maloney directed me here."

Herman knew that new recruits were coming. The major had told him two days ago. The major who had watched half of his men die in Gallipoli had aged ten years in the seven months. He had been in Gallipoli, but being Australian, he had no voice in any of the operations.

"Grab a mattress," Herman invited as he surveyed the new recruit. He was a stocky lad about five feet eight inches tall, blonde curly hair and blue eyes that peeped through slits when he smiled.

"Where are you from Paul?" Herman asked.

"Northam. We ran five thousand acres of wheat and sheep," was the enthusiastic reply.

The conversation was interrupted as new recruits filled up tent 14 and 13. Jack Clare was a drover and shearer from Meekatharra. Six foot four and shoulders two axe handles wide. Jacky Ryan came from Kojunup and was a sheep farmer. Bernie Ring a short gymnastics instructor was from Perth. He was perky and walked with a sort of a hop. He looked as if he was a hunchback but it was all muscle. Maurice Quirke, tall with spikey straw hair from Albany completed the boarders of tent 13. The other tent housed Basil Hickey, a serious farmer from Moora, Smiley Mick Heathorne from Mandurah and Kev Morton from Dongara. Remo (Mick) Genetti from Orange Grove was an Italian wine maker while Brendan Duffy was a tall, slim farmer from the Swan Valley and John O'Halloran was a bandy legged, snow-white blonde from Fremantle.

"Are you an albino?" Mick Genetti asked.

Jack O'Halloran laughed and turned red.

"Better than being an Italian wineo," he replied. And then it was on for one and all.

Mick's fiery temper rose to explosive heat. He threw a boot and followed with a flying tackle. Basil Hickey came to Jack's assistance. Mick Heathorne couldn't make up his mind so fought against both sides. Brendan Duffy laughed and pushed the tangled mess of humanity from one part of the tent to the other. Kev Morton, the opening batsman for Greenough Flats who always made a century, lay on a pile of Bedouin cushions and went to sleep. Herman upon hearing the ruckus stuck his head under the tent flap.

"Billy's on," he said. "We are throwing in a touch of rum to get the cobwebs away."

Tempers immediately were dissipated and uncontrollable laughter followed. Over the cuppa and smoke, the men talked of their experiences and their short history. Paul Flanagan was the youngest at eighteen and Jack Clare was the golden oldie at twenty years of age. New friends and the daily routine soon took away the pain of the loss that Herman suffered following the Gallipoli fiasco.

In Europe the war was going badly for the Allies. Of the 222,000 Australians overseas, only 42,424 remained with the Egyptian Expeditionary Forces. They were part of the fourteen divisions placed under the command of General Sir Archibald Murray, "Old Archie" as he was lovingly called by his troops. He was the new Commander in Chief. He had taken over from Sir John Maxwell. The Anzac Mounted Divisions included Scottish and English Cavalry as well as the 1st, 2nd and 3rd Light Horse Brigades, the New Zealand Mounted Rifle Brigades and the Royal Horse Artillery Brigade of Inverness, Ayrshire and Somerset batteries. General Harry Chauvel was in command of all the Anzac Mounted Divisions. These were all moved to one large camp in the vicinity of Kantara, a small town between Port Said and Ishmailia. It was on the eastern side of the Suez Canal and the extreme western edge of the Sinai Desert on a tiny bridge of land between two lakes. The large Northern Lake was Lake Manzaleh and the lake to the south was Lake Balah. This town had seen traders pass through it since the time of Moses. Napoleon had passed through as had the Babylonians, Assyrians, Persians,

Greeks and the Crusades. It was the land entrance to the Sinai Desert and the glorious cities of the East. For the Turks, however, it was the entrance to Egypt.

Fresh from the victories at Gallipoli, the Turks turned their attention to boundaries on the east near Russia and the south near Egypt. A small attack on the Suez Canal had been turned back on the 3rd of February 1915. The Turks had therefore withdrawn to Palestine and Syria, leaving small patrols in some villages, which were of strategic value. But with victory in Gallipoli, swiftly reinforcements were brought to Gaza by train. From here all that remained was a mere 150-mile trek across the top of Sinai into Egypt. However the terrain was inhospitable and the enthusiast British Air force stationed at Moascar surveyed the old coastal trade road constantly.

When the members of tent 13 and 14 moved into Kantara, they retained their tent number, but they found themselves part of another large canvas city. Each day the members of the 10th Light Horse had to go on patrols into the desert. Some of the dunes reached to 400 feet high and when the horses slid down the sides of these monsters they were virtually up to their bellies in sand. The men had to participate in the trench digging exercises. This was difficult in the bottomless sand pit. The trenches were wide and the walls were maintained with sand bags.

The engineers began building a railway line from Kantara along the side of the century old caravan road to Gaza. The lines were being laid at the rate of 13 miles per month. The Egyptian farmers who tilled the fertile soil along the Nile were called *'Fellahin'*. and were forced into labour gangs to lay the railway line. Over 120,000 fellahin worked on this line and were fed by the local peasants and farmers whose corn, fodder, camels and donkeys were requisitioned. All the materials for the railway were brought from England. The ships had to encounter the continuous hazards of the German submarines. As the railway pushed forward so did the trenches and the tent cities. During the months of January, February and March, all was quiet.

Recreation was taken in Cairo. The Ghezira Club's tennis courts had been used as a temporary hospital following the landing at Gallipoli but it was not long before suitable accommodation was found for the wounded or they were sent home or conveniently died. The Ghezirah club returned to being the major attraction for the officers. On the courts, tea, strawberries and cucumber sandwiches were the order of the day as the ladies giggled and swayed their way among the British officers who had taken up residence in most of the hotels. The Australians thought they could drink anywhere that served beer but the British officers thought otherwise. The Shepheard's Hotel Long Bar was banned to the lower ranks. British officers could not handle the Australians casual attitude and the fact that Australians thought they were equal to all British military personnel.

"What do you mean I can't go into the bar?" asked Jackie Ryan as he stood in the foyer of the Shepheard's Hotel.

"This bar is reserved for the officers of the British Army," said the concierge of the hotel dressed in native costume with a red fez adorning his head.

"Well I'm a bloody officer of the British army mate," retorted Jackie Ryan.

"Sir, you are a mere trooper of the Australian Light Horse. I know the uniform and the black and gold colour patch indicates you are from the 10th Light Horse. I know my colour patches," replied the concierge with a delightful smile.

"Well do you recognize a bloody Aussie fist," said Jackie and punched him on the nose sending him reeling to the floor.

"Come on lads the beers are on me,"

The members of tent 13 and 14 walked into the bar and had sufficient time to help themselves to a beer before being forcibly removed by the military police. Charges were laid but the papers were torn up by Major Maloney.

"I simply call it a public relations exercise," he explained to the British officer laying the complaint.

The Ghezirah Club had a racetrack and here the 10th excelled. They entered their own horses in the weekly race meetings, which were held every Saturday in the cooler months from September to March. Some of the horses that won included Colonel Todd's *'Babanooka'*, which won four races in succession. Lieutenant Norrish's *'Kojonup'* was a regular winner, Lieutenant MacDonald's *'Old Nick'* was well favoured and Major Olden's *'Yaboo'* and *'Orchardor'* were well backed for a win or place.

Despite the race meetings, the cricket and football matches, the Aussies knew that within that hot God forsaken desert Johnny Turk was ever present.

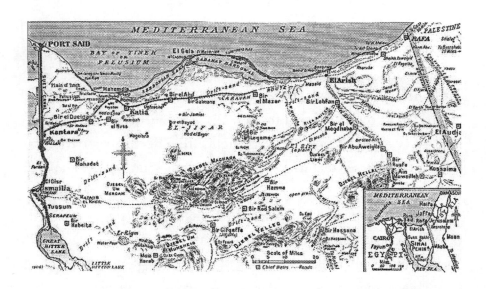

Fig. 9. Map of the Northern Sinai in 1916

Chapter 14: Johnny Turk

Mehemet Ohman was the son of a carpet dealer. Although he was eighteen he was already a veteran. He had endured the hardships of Gallipoli. He had charged with his bayonet fixed to his rifle when Mustafa Kemal had ordered him to charge.

"I don't order you to fight. I order you to die. In the time it takes us to die, other troops and commanders will come to take our place. You are fighting for your faith. Death is martyrdom. The sword is the key to Heaven and Hell."

The words of his leader kept ringing in his ears as he defended the Gallipoli plateau.

He had stood in trenches and fired his rifle as the Anzacs came ashore in Gallipoli. For almost six months he had sat in a trench only twelve yards from the Aussie trenches. He had heard them laugh. He knew their familiar flat toned voices. He had fired at them during action times and exchanged cigarettes with them during respite times. He had watched the Anzacs leave his shores. Now he was walking along the well-trodden road from Gaza to Kantara with a force of 25,000 Austrian and Turkish troops. Their mission was to take Romani. From here they could use artillery to snipe at any ships using the Suez Canal, which was a mere twenty-three miles away. Their commander, Kress von Kressenstein, had chosen to march by night and rest by day. The troops marched on a sixteen-mile front, using both the coastal road and waddies. Where possible they avoided the ever-present sand dunes. Mehemet sat beneath a palm tree as the sun began to rise. He was tired. Flies pestered his salty eyes.

He had attended high school in Constantinople until the war broke out. He had studied History, German, English and Turkish as well as Science, Mathematics. He had enjoyed being in the cadets. He hoped to go to a University in England to complete a degree. But since they were now invading his country he thought maybe Germany would be the place to finish his studies. He wondered about the Australians. Why were they here as part of the British Army? They were tall, tenacious and shouted a lot. He had watched them charge at Nek and even though his fellow Turkish soldiers handling the machine guns had called to them to turn back, they kept coming. This was madness. Now he was marching to take Romani and Australians occupied this place. Mehemet shivered and slept as the hot sun began its daily duty of searing the earth. Flies and fleas took cover in the folds of his uniform.

It was the 17th of July, 1916. It was Herman's birthday. He was twenty years of age. At 4.00 am he flicked back the flap of his tent. Here he was twenty in a tent city at a place called Romani. He looked at the lines of tents that housed almost ten thousand troops. Row upon row of white pointy tents reflected the early morning light. A soft whinny came from one of the horses tethered to the line adjoining his tent. Herman walked to his horse, Peter.
"Good morning mate. It's my birthday today. Are you going to wish me happy birthday?" The horse whinnied happy birthday in deep mellow tones. Herman filled Peter's nosebag with oats.

"Birthday cake," said Herman. He then filled the water troughs with water. All the horses drank to Herman's health.

The tent city and water pipelines had moved with the railway. After several months in the Kantara camp, the troops had moved to Romani. Here the tents were placed on the outskirts of the ancient town. Herman stirred the campfire and threw a few logs on it to boil the billy.

"Billy's boiling," Herman called the members of tent 13. It was 5.00 am and the railway workers were already laying sleepers and track. The sound of the sledgehammers on the rail bolts echoed through the camp.

"Don't those buggers ever stop?" grumped Maurice Quirk as he rolled out of his blanket on the ground and filled his pannikin with the life saving brew. Bernie Ring popped around the corner of the tent having relieved himself in the desert.

"If you didn't have ears, Bernie, your hat would cover your whole head," Remo Genetti quipped referring to Bernie's somewhat diminutive head.

"It's better than having a head that is so big nothing fits on it or in it," Bernie remarked. All laughed heartily and enjoyed the joke.

By seven o'clock they were dressed, saddled, armed and ready. The 10th Regiment as always headed the reconnaissance patrol. The Regimental Song was *'Marching through Georgia,'* adapted to local conditions and places. Major Maloney was in the leading four, which included Herman Murphy, Jackie Clare and Maurice Quirke. The next four were Paul Flanagan, Jackie Ryan, Bernie Ring, and Basil Hickey. Then came Remo Genetti, Mick Heathorne, Brendan Duffy as a three and behind them Jack O'Halloran and Kev Morton who was asleep in the saddle. Behind the men of tent 13 and 14 were some of the biggest larrikins to ever leave West Australia.

"Give me a cadence trooper," Major Maloney ordered. Paul Flanagan began and all joined in.

There were no road signs to show the way. The desert sands were ever changing. The Kantara-Gaza road was well trodden however and was easy to follow. Off the road the Oasis Villages were hard to find. Herman was the pathfinder. He had a natural sense of direction. It was as if he had a map in his brain. Their task on this patrol was to occupy Katia before the Turks got there. Katia was a small village on the main road some six miles south east of Romani. Aerial reconnaissance had put the Turks some twenty miles from the desert town. So the men sang merrily and settled into a short ride to a friendly Oasis Village.

General Archibald Murray who was in charge of the Egypt Expeditionary Force was expecting an attack on Romani. He had therefore strengthened his position. General Sir H.A. Lawrence was in charge of the Northern Canal Defence. He had the 52nd British Infantry Division positioned on the east of Romani. They were entrenched with strategically placed redoubts. He had the New Zealand Mounted Rifles and the 5th Mounted Brigade entrenched on the west around Mt. Royston and to the south on Wellington Ridge. These were under the command of General Chaytor. So Romani was secure and Chauvel's Mounted Division patrolled the oases and villages to the east and south.

"You know Murph, I've never shot a real person only dummies," said Paul as they rocked rhythmically in the saddle.

"Didn't they tell you, you are not supposed to shoot British generals? They're the only dummies I know," Maurice Quirk joked.

"I don't think any of us have shot a real person on purpose. Those blokes who went to Gallipoli did, but there aren't many of those left in the 10ᵗʰ," Herman added sombrely.

The men rode quietly. Chauvel called a halt about half a mile from the outskirts of Katia. They were protected by the surrounding sand dunes. Chauvel with his supporting team took high ground where they could observe the town.

"Damn reconnaissance," he said. "The town's crawling with Turks." Together the team evaluated the strength of the enemy and the machine gun mountings.

"There's no artillery Sir," observed one of the majors.

"They would be on a hill well out of town," observed another.

"They could then pound us to pieces if we take the town. That's it then, *'Strike but Strike Quickly,'* so they don't know what hit them. Have our machine guns mounted on the perimeter and when in position we'll let 'em have it."

The men tethered their horses, leaving a trooper in charge of ten horses a piece. It took only an hour for the men to be in place.

"Let's serve them lead for breakfast lads. Remember Nek," Major Maloney ordered.

Mehemet was drinking a well-earned cup of coffee when the first spray of bullets hit the date palm. The young dates in the palm dropped upon him in a shower of green rain. Birds collecting insects around the palm scattered. The whole town awoke with the hysterical screams of lethal weapons. The tenacious Turks quickly swung into action, taking cover where they could and returned fire.

The machine guns barked and the rifles spat death at the intruders. The strange sounds caused the desert foxes to hide and whimper.

By ten o'clock Paul Flanagan had shot two trees and four tents. Bernie Ring had shot a chicken and a turkey. Herman sat behind a machine gun and rattled it in a steady arc while Jackie Clare fed the ammunition and monitored the temperature of the gun. They swept through five enemy machine gun mounts and considered they had been successful because no movement came from that area. The order was given to fix bayonets.

"Shit," said Paul Flanagan. "I was enjoying the war up to now."

"Take your hat off Bernie," joked Maurice Quirke, "You might trip over the chin strap." Bernie's eyes were red. He had been taken by some force within his brain that had turned him into a ferocious being and with a rifle and a bayonet that was a dangerous combination.

"Just joking," Maurice retracted his joke. "Let's go."

With one almighty shout some two thousand men charged down the hillside. Mehemet had heard that cry before. He was relieved to hear the order to retreat.

"That wasn't so bad," Paul Flanagan commented as he sat under a palm tree enjoying a smoke one hour later. "How did you go Bernie?"

Adrenaline poured out of the young soldier as he relieved himself in a nearby bush. He returned.

"How are you mate?" asked Maurice who noticed the fanatic frenzy had passed.

"Good, bloody good. They just ran away,"

"I am not surprised," Maurice thought to himself.

Then it happened. First a whole palm tree disappeared; them a village mud hut, then a well blew up and sprayed its contents like a spring shower over the resting Aussies. It was the Turks turn. Artillery first, followed by a charge of the infantry. A lot of infantry! More infantry than the Aussies could match. After several hours Chauval ordered a withdrawal. The Turks had taken Katia back.

"Hey Murph want to go for a ride?" Major Maloney asked, "We've lost communication with Romani. Will you go and report the situation and call for reinforcements. Here I've written it down. Don't waste any time. We have to take this town."

Herman slipped from behind the machine gun and gave it to Maurice Quirke. He ran the half-mile to the tethered horses. Peter was standing quietly with his head down. He lifted it and pricked his ears when he heard his mate's low whistle. He gave a deep mumble of greeting.

"We've got to go for a bit of a ride mate," Herman whispered as he tightened the girth several notches and swung into the saddle. Peter needed no urging. He skied down the dunes until he hit the solid ground of the wadi and took off at a gallop. "Pace yourself mate we have five miles to go. Think of it as the Melbourne Cup," Herman whispered.

Man and beast worked as one as they crossed the stony waddies which hadn't tasted water for many years. Peter stormed up the fine-sanded dunes and skied down the other side. He galloped into Romani. Steam rose from Peter as he waited impatiently outside the commanding officer's quarters.

While the 1st and 2nd Light Horse Brigade, and the New Zealand Mounted Rifles men made ready, Herman went to the water trough

99

filled his hat with water and gave his mount a steady drink whispering congratulatory words into his ear. One hour later the two thousand mounted fighting men were on the road to Katia.

"What've you been doing while we were away?" Herman asked as he relieved Maurice Quirk from behind the machine gun.

"Sunbaking," replied the exhausted Quirke.

The Mounted Artillery Brigade began the afternoon session with a series of musical bombings. The Australian Air Command flew overhead and dropped several explosive messages. The machine guns took up the theme and peppered the town of Katia with a monotonous one-note waltz and then the Aussies charged with bayonets fixed.

Kress von Kressenstein withdrew to Oghretina ten miles East of Katia.

"Run rabbit run rabbit run,run run. We'll get you. We'll get you with our gun, gun, gun," Herman sang as he uncocked his machine gun but held his post.

"Do you think they'll be back?" asked Jackie Clare giving deference to the younger but more experience mate.

"I would say they will go to the next village and lick their wounds. They won't be back today. But they'll be back. If they cut off the Suez, they cut off the main British supply line. That's their plan and Johnny Turk won't give up easily." Several regiments were left in Katia when the main body of troops withdrew to Romani. Kress von Kressenstein lay quietly at Oghretina and slowly built up his reinforcements for a major onslaught on Romani.

Light Horse patrols went out every night just to see where Johnny Turk was and what mischief he was up to.

"I reckon they are up to no good," said Basil Hickey who was lying on the sand dune some three hundred yards from Oghretina.

"I bet they have troops in every wadi further south," suggested Herman.

"Let's check," said Major Maloney.

The men slid down the dune to where their horses were tethered.

They rode along the wadi for an hour and then climbed the sand dune to survey the area. In the moonlight shadowy clumps stood out.

"They're bloody cannons," said Major Maloney. "Old Johnny Turk has his heart set on Romani."

"They'll come in from the south," said Basil Hickey.

"Maybe they will come in all directions. They really want Romani. It makes sense. From there they can drop shells on the ships using the canal."

The men continued riding through the night and by sunrise they were at Bir al Nuss; a large oasis directly south of Romani.

"Well glory be. Looky here," said Basil Hickey.

"I'd say about twenty cannon and five thousand troops down there. What do you think Murph?" Major Maloney asked.

"More like ten major," replied Herman.

The sun had started its rise. The temperature was a hundred degrees Fahrenheit and it was only six in the morning. Buoyed on by adrenaline, the patrol returned to Romani. Here they delivered their information.

"I thought they would launch an attack from the South," said General H. A. Lawrence, the Commander of the Northern Suez defence.

"My divisions are mobile, so we could draw Johnny Turk from the south and then he is caught between your East and West infantry and artillery. After they have finished with him, my Light Horse could strike," suggested Chauvel.

The plan was put into practice.

On the night of August the 3rd as the 2nd Light Horse Brigade was returning to Romani from a reconnaissance patrol, a force of 8,000 Turks followed them. Having detected that the attack was imminent Chauvel had positioned the 1st Light Horse Brigade on a loose defensive line running from Katib Gannit at the southern tip of the infantry entrenchment heading southwest along the edge of the sand hills, passing through a large sand hill called Mount Meredith and ending at Hod el Enna.

Though vastly outnumbered, the light horsemen fought an effective delaying action at close quarters. They relinquished ground slowly. Around 2.30 am on August the 4th after the moon had set, the Turks made a bayonet charge on Mount Meredith and the Light Horse evacuated the position at 3.00 am. The Australians were eventually forced back to a large east-west sand dune called Wellington Ridge at the southern edge of the Romani encampment. Having been held south of Romani, the Turks attempted a further outflanking manoeuvre to the west and concentrate 2000 troops around another sand hill called Mount Royston, southwest of Romani.

At dawn Chauvel sent the 2nd Light Horse Brigade into action in front of Mount Royston. The Turkish advance was at a standstill everywhere. After a long night march the Turkish troops now faced a difficult day under the desert sun without a source of water and exposed to the main artillery. Shortly after dawn the Turks succeeded in forcing the Australians off Wellington Ridge, which placed them within 700 yards of the Romani camp. However they were depleted, exhausted and exposed to shelling from horse artillery so they were unable to press the attack further.

Then Chaytor's brigades launched a counter attack. The Turks at Mount Royston were checked to the north by the 3rd and 6th Light Horse regiments. They were under bombardment from the horse artillery and the heavy artillery of the 52nd Division and when Chaytor's force attacked from the west, Turks surrendered *en masse* around 6.00 pm on August the 4th.

Both sides rested that night.

At dawn on August the 5th the Australian Light Horse Regiments and the New Zealand Mounted Rifles Regiment, led by the 10th mounted an attack on the remaining Turkish positions and by 5.00 am had captured 1,000 prisoners and driven off the remainder. Everywhere along the front, the Turks were either surrendering or retreating. An opportunity to encircle and annihilate the retreating Turks west of Katia was missed when the 52nd Division failed to advance promptly to coincide with the recapture of Wellington Ridge. The New Zealand 1st and 2nd Light Horse and 5th Mounted Brigades attacked the Turks at Katia at 3.30 pm on August the 5th but were unable to dislodge them. Chauvel ordered a withdrawal back to Romani. Some of the Light Horse had been in constant combat for 59 hours.

The Turks however were retreating their entire force from Katia to Oghratina and then to Bir el Abd. By August 12th the Turks had evacuated Bir el Abd and ultimately retreated to El Arish from where they began their original advance. By the time the Turks were driven out of Katia their casualties were 1,250 dead and an estimated

4,000 wounded. The British had taken 1,950 prisoners. Total British casualties were 1,130 of which 202 were killed.

While the railway was pushing towards El Arish at roughly 10 miles per month, gold arms and supplies were being delivered to Sherif Hussein who had raised the flag of revolt on the 16th of June 1915. In October 1915 English officers, including Lawrence, arrived to assist Hussein and keep the Arab Revolt on the boil. Lawrence with his spectacular guerrilla tactics began to move northwards from the Hejaz zone and the Holy cities of Medina and Mecca.

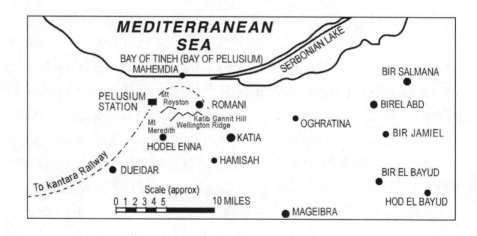

Fig.10. Battle of Romani

Chapter 15: The Battle of Magdhaba

Following the victory at Romani, General Sir Archibald Murray shifted his headquarters from Ismailia to the Savoy Hotel in Cairo and put all the troops east of the Suez Canal under the command of Major General C. M. Dobell who despite lack of experience, received a promotion to lieutenant general. Lieutenant General Sir Phillip Cherwood was made General Officer Commanding of the Desert Column. He had difficulty with the Australians.

"Those men of yours," he confided in Harry Chauvel. "They don't salute me and they laugh at my orderlies. Can they fight in battle?"

"They can hold their own," replied Harry euphemistically.

The hot summer came to an end. With September came days that were cooler. The railway was progressing, the troops were patrolling the desert and the officers were lounging in the Shepheard's Hotel in Cairo.

"Those Australians are a disgrace to the British Army," said Colonel Fotheringham Jones in his best Eton College accent to his fellow officer Colonel Billingsworth as he sipped his gin and tonic in the Long Bar.

"The best thing, old chap, is to avoid them. Make sure they don't come between the wind and you. They do have a strange smell," was the educated reply.

"Anyway what is this latest order from the O.C. on Dress and Deportment, *'All Officers should ensure their socks match the rest of their clothing.'* I thought that would have been common practice and hardly warrant an order."

"Australians again old chap. Since Gallipoli some of those colonials have been promoted. They have no sense of dress code. I saw an Australian major wearing tartan socks in full dress uniform. No idea whatsoever. We should leave them out of the next war. Another drink old chap?"

"Thanks old chap. This October weather has a bit of a chill about it during the evening."

Three days later looking resplendent in his major's uniform, *'Major for a night'* Trooper Basil Hickey appeared at the door of the Long Bar. He was flanked by two junior officers, Lieutenant Heathorne who had managed to control his smile, and Lieutenant Brendan Duffy.

"Attention! Officer Commanding to conduct sock inspection," shouted Brendan Duffy in an officious voice.

"According to Order 2351, in the name of proper dress and deportment all officers should at all times wear socks that match the rest of their dress," shouted Smiley Heathorne. "Would all members present, prepare for sock inspection. Remove both right and left boot or shoe and raise both feet to display socks." There were lots of *'By Joves'* and *'Jolly Goods'* resounding throughout the Bar but all present took off their boots and displayed their socks. There was a thorough inspection with *'umms'* and *'rrs'* by the temporary, in clandestine *Officers for Dress and Deportment*. When the inspection was complete the three stood at the entrance, saluted and Major Hickey shouted authoritatively. "Carry on," and left the Long Bar.

Members of tent 14 and 13 greeted him at the entrance to the Shepheard's Hotel and they proceeded to the tram terminus to catch a tram for Heliopolis as a ban had been placed on Australian troops entering Cairo. This was disciplinary because of several riots that had occurred following conflict between the Australians and the English. After five days leave the temporary officers and their entourage returned to Romani and the real war.

The Turks occupied El Arish an Oasis on the old caravan road about one mile in from the coast. They also occupied Bir al Magdhaba, some 18 miles along the Wadi Arish, which ran south from El Arish. Magdhaba is on the banks of the Wadi el Arish. It was a central point of movement across the Sinai Peninsula. Mehemet was one of the 4,000 Turkish soldiers who was positioned there. Although he was not Christian he knew that the 25th of December was a sacred day for the Christians. He, like many others had wrongly assumed the British forces would not attack their stronghold. Telegraphed messages informed the Turkish High Command at Magdhaba that El Arish had fallen so they prepared for an attack.

At 10.00 am on the 23rd of December 1915. Mehemet was on duty in the long line of trenches that had been dug into the chalky bottom of the Wadi. Cannon fire began from the British cannons. When the cannons stopped the machine guns began their deathly *rat a tat tat* into the flat chalky stronghold. Overhead, planes flew. Bombs were dropped by the co pilot who then fired on the troops with his Lewis gun. Then an extraordinary sight appeared four hundred yards in front of him. Men on horseback came charging towards him. They held their rifles fixed with bayonets and using them as lances, charged towards him. He fired several rounds then turned to his companion next to him. Fear was in his eyes. The horses kept coming ignoring the gunfire. To run was foolish; to stay was even more foolish. His commander tied a white handkerchief to the end of his bayonet and raised it high signifying surrender.

The charge of the 10th had secured Magdhaba by the end of the day. The Desert Column withdrew as there was insufficient water because the Turks had blown up some of the wells.

After riding all night the 10th, as part of the 3rd Brigade, reached Hod Masaid at 8.30 am on the 24th of December. Here, there was a plentiful supply of water.

"This will be your home for a few weeks," Major Maloney informed his men. "There are extra rations for you all. Happy Christmas."

"He's a nice boy," said Kev Morton who rolled out his blanket curled up in it like a worm in a cocoon and went to sleep. His horse stood over him while he slept. Herman collected the horse and took it and Peter to a nearby palm grove. There was grass underfoot. He took the saddles off and rubbed the horses down and like the rest of the 10th found a spot next to his mates and curled up in his blanket.

"Hey Murph where is Bethlehem from here?" asked Paul Flanagan.

"North East about 200 miles. Why?" Herman responded.

"I think I can see the star that settles over the stable,"

Paul had a deep baritone voice and he began to sing *Silent Night*. Basil Hickey with his strong tenor voice joined in harmony and Bernie Ring brought out his mouth organ and gave the carol a sombre backing. The men joined in.

Back at Magdhaba, Mehemet celebrated his first Christian Christmas in the confines of the makeshift prison. His war was over.

"Does Australia have a university?" he thought.

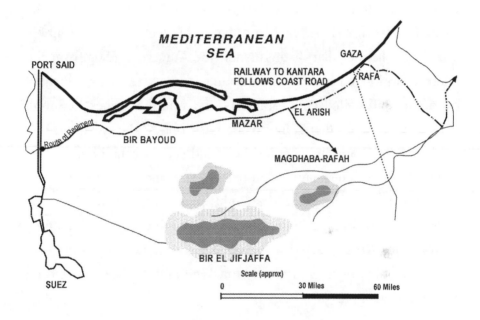

Fig.11. Map of the Battles of Sinai.

Chapter 16: The Battle of Rafa

Mustafa Kemit was wakened by the cold of the morning. He reached into his uniform pocket and looked at the watch his father had given him for his fifteenth birthday two years ago. It was 3.30 am on the 9th of January 1917. He reached down to his feet and picked up his khaki pith helmet that distinguished the Turkish soldier from the enemy. He looked around his redoubt. It was one of four located on a bare hill called Hill 255. This one was the highest redoubt. There were three others, one to the east, one to the west and one to the south. From this position he could see the small oasis of El Magruntein, which snuggled against the surrounding barren hills the colour of his uniform. The first light of dawn began to silver the hillside and the Prussian blue sky was lightening slightly. His three companions were asleep, even Osama who was keeping watch had dozed off, his fingers still on the machine gun. His head rested on the butt of the gun.

Mustafa lit a cigarette. "You're too young to smoke," he heard the voice of his mother in his mind's memory. "It will turn your beautiful white teeth yellow. Look at your father's." He loved his parents, especially his mother. She had cried when he left for Gallipoli and cried when he returned and cried when he embarked on the train at Constantinople for Egypt.

"That is not our land. There is no need to fight there," she had argued with a mother's protective logic. He was her handsome son who one day would be a tour guide showing people over the ancient cities of

Troy where the Turks had stood strong against all assailants except the Greeks bearing gifts.

"Never trust a Greek," she would say. Yes a tour guide would be fun but now there were two Troys; one on each side of the Dardanelles. He hated Gallipoli. For eight months he had sat in a trench merely eight yards from the enemy. He had talked to these strange "Aussie blokes" who were willing to share their cigarettes with them while there was a cease-fire. He remembered them withdrawing and Mustafa Kemal had given the order. *"A retreating man is not to be shot."* But here on the Sinai Peninsula it was a different Aussie. He rode the horse and seemed fearless on the open plain. He was more Bedouin than the Bedouin. They called them *'Billjims'*. They would scrounge and take anything that was not guarded. Very different from the men he knew.

From his position he could just make out the Mediterranean on the other side of Rafa, a small trading village of no more than 600 occupants. Its numbers had been swelled by the Turkish army that had withdrawn from El Arish. It was the first town on the coastal border. Next stop was Gaza.

Mustafa slowly nodded off to sleep.

Chauvel and Chetwode had set out on the evening of the 8th of January, 1917. They led the 1st Light Horse Brigade, the 3rd Light Horse Brigade and the New Zealand Mounted Rifles. The British 5th Yeomanry Brigade and three battalions of Imperial Camel Corps accompanied them. The 10th Light Horse Regiment was part of the 3rd Brigade.

"Give us a cadence trooper," said Major Maloney to trooper Flanagan as the men of the 10th began their journey into battle.

'Tip toe, through the sand dunes, through the sand dunes, through the sand dunes
Let's tip toe through the sand dunes with me," Paul commenced mockingly to the tune of *Tip Toe Through the Tulips*

"We'll have a serious note trooper," Major Maloney who had grown used to the light-hearted comradery of the 10th.

Paul hit the note perfectly for the Regiment's Song:

Marching through Georgia

Verse 1
Bring the good old bugle, boys, we'll sing another song
Sing it with a spirit that will start the world along
Sing it as we used to sing it, 50,000 strong
While we were marching through Georgia.

Chorus
Hurrah! Hurrah! We bring the jubilee!
Hurrah! Hurrah! the flag that makes you free!
So we sang the chorus from Atlanta to the sea
While we were marching through Georgia.

Verse 2
How the darkies shouted when they heard the joyful sound
How the turkeys gobbled which our commissary found
How the sweet potatoes even started from the ground
While we were marching through Georgia.

Verse 3
Yes and there were Union men who wept with joyful tears,

When they saw the honored flag they had not seen for years;
Hardly could they be restrained from breaking forth in cheers,
While we were marching through Georgia.

Verse 4

"Sherman's dashing Yankee boys will never make the coast!"
So the saucy rebels said and 'twas a handsome boast
Had they not forgot, alas! to reckon with the Host
While we were marching through Georgia.

Verse 5

So we made a thoroughfare for freedom and her train,
Sixty miles of latitude, three hundred to the main;
Treason fled before us, for resistance was in vain
While we were marching through Georgia.

One thousand horsemen picked up the tune. The jackals joined in.

Then all fell silent as each man communicated with his own thoughts. The only sound was the deep rumble of the six Ford cars of the British 7th Light Car Regiment, which supported the yeomanry. Each car carried a machine gun.

At 3.00 am on the 9th of January, Chauvel ordered the New Zealand horsemen to circle south and come in from the east and the north. The 1st Brigade and the Camel Corps came in from the east and south. The 3rd were kept in reserve.

"Did you bring a footy?" Bernie Ring asked Herman as they sat on the gravelly desert sand some two miles west of Rafa. "While we are in reserve we could have a dob or two."

"No such luck but you could do a bit of fish'n if you want. I reckon there would be a few mullet in that sea," replied Herman indicating the Mediterranean some three miles away. "Fried fish for breakfast. Beautiful. Do you know every Christmas my dad and my brothers and sisters would go to Coronation Beach near our farm? The Indian Ocean was alive with fish."

"You didn't need a net or line you just picked them up with your hand," chimed in Jackie Clare.

"No you took the pan down and they jumped right in," said Remo Genetti.

"Pretty much," said Herman.

Then the British Light Horse Artillery opened up with a roar that sent the ears ringing.

"Bloody hell! What was that?" said Kev Morton who had gone to sleep in his horses shadow.

"Go back to sleep Kev. We are in reserve," Basil Hickey explained. "Don't tell him to do that. His snoring is worse than the artillery," laughed Smiley Heathorne.

At 10.00 am a group of Turks left and headed for Gaza. At 11.00 am the infantry advanced to within a mile of the redoubts but the Turks were in a good position as they had high ground and had a clear view of the enemy. As the day wore on the artillery ran out of ammunition, as did the New Zealand Rifle Brigade.

"There go the poms," said Basil Hickey as the Light Horse Artillery hitched up the horses and withdrew from the field.

"Out of ammo," said Brendan Duffy rolling a cigarette and getting ready to boil the billy. It was four o'clock in the afternoon.

"Chetwode has given the order to withdraw. Our aerial reconnaissance has observed Turkish reinforcements advancing towards Rafa," Major Maloney informed his men.

"Hold on. Countermand that," said the major as he listened into the field phone. "The Kiwis have fixed bayonets and are charging the east and south redoubt."

"Bloody New Zealanders! If they had a brain they'd be dangerous," said Kev Morton as he woke up when he smelt the billy boiling.

"Mount up lads," Major Maloney ordered. "We are bringing in the reserves."

Mustafa Kemit was tired but overjoyed because he knew; they had won the day when he saw the Horse Artillery withdraw. They had the high ground and the continual cannon fire had not damaged their redoubt at all. He scanned the horizon through his field glasses. In the east he could see the horsemen fixing their bayonets.

"They are out of ammunition also," he thought.

He spun around to the northwest and he saw almost five thousand horsemen riding at a fast canter. Despite the firing from the redoubt those horsemen kept approaching.

Bernie Ring sat steadily on his horse and then stood in the stirrups.

He fired.

The bullet went straight through Mustafa's pith helmet into his skull and exited coming to rest in the sandbagged wall. Mustafa's ambitions trickled down his forehead. His mother dropped a cup. It smashed on the tiled floor of her tidy home. She knew her son was dead and she cried.

"I think I got him," said Bernie.

The battle was won. Night fell and the score was: The British 71 killed and 415 wounded while the Turks lost about 200 killed, 168 wounded and 1,434 prisoners.

The remaining Turkish garrisons in the Sinai at El Hassana (near Magdhaba) and Nekhl were captured or expelled in mid-February. The fate of the garrisons at Magdhaba and Rafa made the Turks wary of leaving isolated troops at the mercy of the Desert Column.

Chauvel received a knight hood for his outstanding strategy in this the battle of Rafa; many young men received the quietness of the grave.

Next Gaza.

Chapter 17: The First Battle of Gaza

Colonel Billingsworth looked at his highly polished shoes. There was a smudge on the toe.

"How did that get there?" he muttered to himself. "Corporal," he called to the passing waiter. "Give the shoes a bit of a buff up. There's a good chap."

The corporal put down his tray and took a cloth from his waist and buffed up the colonel's shoes. The corporal was a waiter in the Long Bar in the Shepheard's Hotel. This bar was reserved for British officers.

"Just open the window a tad. Let the afternoon breeze in. Quite hot for March. What do think Jones?" Billingsworth asked his companion.

"It's the end of March old chap so one can expect the temperature to be around the 100 mark. Another gin and tonic please corporal and make it a little colder," responded Colonel Fotheringham-Jones. A man in his fifties of whom Gilbert and Sullivan could have written. *"If you want to get to the top of the tree . . . . Never go to war. Just polish up the handle of the big front door."* He was in personal and human relations as was Colonel Billingsworth. Neither had fired a shot in anger.

"Dobell and his crowd are having a go at Gaza as I speak," said Billingsworth looking at his watch.

"Should be over by tea I would say. According to reports the Turks and the Austrians in Gaza are well under strength," Jones added.

"It's those confounded Anzacs. They seem to be able to ride all night and fight all day. There's no accounting for it. Their horses are the same. It's the wild colonial thing. No breeding. Corporal a refill please!"

In the field of battle the drinks being served were a little different.

"Hey Bernie! Have you got any water left in your bottle? My mouth just needs a touch. A bullet put a hole in mine," Herman explained as he looked down on the city of Gaza.

"What?" asked Bernie. "I can't hear a thing with those planes and cannons jumping all over the place."

"Doesn't matter," Herman shook his head and decided to go dry.

The sun was setting over the Mediterranean. The Anzacs had completed their mission. They had commenced under cover of fog at 2.00 am on the 26th of March. They had circled the surrounding hills and after a short period of fighting had taken the summit of Ali Muntar where Samson many centuries before had fought the Philistines with the jawbone of an ass. They were now dismounted in a cactus forest just north of Gaza. Bad communication and delays had turned this battle into a fiasco.

"Mount up lads," Major Maloney ordered.

"We are charging into the city?" Jackie Ryan smiled revealing a broken tooth.

"Retreating,"

"What! But the city is ours Mal," protested Herman in anger. He was thirsty.

"Those are orders. Brigadier General Ryrie asked for the order in writing and got it from Dobell and Chetwode.

"They got nuts for brains or what?" asked Jackie Clare as he swung into the saddle. The British forces out numbered the Turks two to one. A force of 22,000 had attacked a force of 15,000. The British lost 4,000 men either killed or wounded but the Turks lost 2,447.

Kress von Kressenstein watched the troops withdraw. "What are they doing?" he asked.

"Retreating," responded General Talia Bey, the nominal Turkish Commander of Gaza.

"That is foolish. They have missed their opportunity for victory. I was about to withdraw. General! Call up reserves from Beersheba. We will beat the British this time."

During the night 4,000 Turkish troops joined their comrades in Gaza. At first light on the 27th of March the battle resumed but lack of supplies and water resulted in the British ordering a complete withdrawal.

"What was that all about?" Basil Hickey asked as he joined the column on its retreat across the sandy valley.

"I think an exercise," said Mick Genetti as he rolled a cigarette. "Anyway I just came for the trip. I have never seen Gaza before."

"Well what did you think?" asked Kev Morton yawning.

"It's a nice place but I wouldn't live there," was the Italian's reply. The men slept in the saddle as they withdrew to Wadi Ghuzze five miles along the coastal road. This town was on the edge of the desert and had luxuriant plantations of figs, almonds and lemons. The fields were bright with flowers and fields of wheat and barley. The horses enjoyed the relief from the battlefield.

General Archibald Murray sent an optimistic and ambiguous account of the battle, which misled the war cabinet and convinced them that a second attack would be successful. This time the instructions came to advance past Gaza and capture Jerusalem. The British needed a victory to bolster morale. They were losing on the Western Front.

Fig.12. British Army Headquarters in Egypt. 1914-1918

Chapter 18: Second Battle of Gaza

"A cadence gentleman," commanded Major Maloney as the 10th led the troops in the second attack on Gaza.

Paul Flanagan commenced. *"Underneath Old Archie, we'll wait for you; wait for you; wait for you."* He sang mocking the tactics of Sir Archibald Murray in the previous attack on Gaza.

"Respect gentlemen. Respect. I think our cadence begins with *'Bring the good old bugle boys we'll sing another song'."* He commenced in resonant tones, singing the first verse and the men joined in.

'Hurrah! Hurrah! We bring the jubilee!
Hurrah! Hurrah! The flag that makes you free!
So we sang the chorus from Atlanta to the sea
While we were marching through Georgia.'

It was the 17th of April 1917.

Dobell planned a typical western front attack with two days of preliminary bombardment followed by a frontal infantry assault on the enemy trenches. The experienced combat commanders, General Phillip Chetwode, Commander of the British Desert Column, and General Henry Chauvel, Commander of the Anzac Mounted Column, were less optimistic about the chances of breaking the Turkish line.

In fact, on the eve of the attack one British commander concluded his briefing thus:

"That, gentlemen, is the plan, and I might say frankly that I don't think much of it."

It was estimated that the Turkish forces occupying the Gaza-Beersheba defences numbered between 20,000 and 25,000. The defences had been strengthened since the first battle. The west flank of the line was defended by the fortress of Gaza. To the east, the line was held by a series of redoubts located on ridges, with each redoubt providing support for its neighbours. The low ground between the redoubts was unoccupied or lightly held. From west to east these redoubts were *Tank, Atawineh, Hareira and Sheria.* Beyond Sheria the defences were thin as far as the township of Beersheba but the lack of water on the approaches to this region made the Turks consider that only a cavalry raid was likely.

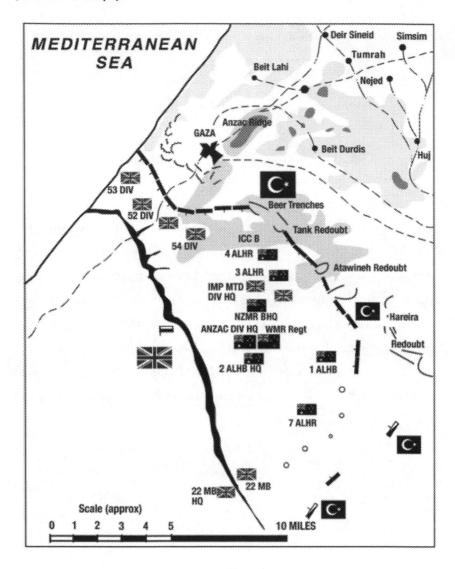

Fig.13. Positions in Second Battle of Gaza at 2.00 pm 19th of April 1917

Bombardment commenced from the three battleships at sea and the British Howitzers. The target was the Turkish defence in the old city and on Ali Muntar. This continued for two days. The infantry moved in, supported by six tanks, which drew the artillery fire from the Turks. Two thousand canisters of poisonous gas were fired by the British. The slight breeze that blew through the valley from Beersheba to Gaza swept the gas out to sea rendering the gas ineffectual.

So when the infantry moved towards Gaza on the morning of the 19th to their horror the Turks were still manning their positions.

"Bloody hell they suppose to be gassed," commented an English infantryman.

The 3rd Light Horse Brigade had begun its advance before dawn and, attacking along the spine of the Atawineh ridge east of Gaza, managed to approach to within 800 yards of the redoubt before being sighted. However, their advance was premature so that the units on their flanks were still well behind. They managed to close to 500 yards during the day but got no further. The 4th Light Horse and 5th Mounted Brigades managed similar advances on their sectors but nowhere were the Turkish trenches reached and given the inferior position of the attackers; there was no prospect of making a successful bayonet charge. The horses had been tethered behind a ridge. The Turkish aeroplanes targeted the horses and began to bomb the easy target.

"The bastards," shouted Maurice Quirk and left his position and took off to save his horse. The rest of the 10th followed him. The squeal of the dying horses combined with the droning of the planes, the cannon fire and the *'rat tat tat'* of the machine guns urged the infuriated men on. The men steadied their horses or put the wounded ones out of their misery.

"Cop a load of that," said Bernie Ring as he looked east towards Beersheba. A huge cloud of dust rose from the sandy valley and it looked as if thousands of horses were riding straight towards the 10th. The Australians hoped they weren't visible and would be able to catch the Turks in crossfire. The charge from Beersheba slowed to reveal the Turkish Cavalry on their beautiful Arab steeds followed by a motley crew of mobile animals, which included donkeys and camels.

The arrival of the Turkish Cavalry was supported by cannon fire, which made the position for the Australians untenable. They withdrew crossing the plain to the highland held by the British. The Turks charged with drawn sword but were repulsed by the British machine gun mounts. The rest of the allied forces retreated. What should have been an easy victory was a terrible defeat. The allies lost at least 6,444 men while the Turks lost only 2,000.

Despondently Paul Flanagan began the cadence on the march back to Wadi Ghuzze.

"The grand old Duke of York. He had ten thousand men.
He marched them to the top of the hill and marched them back again."

All joined in.

"And when they were up, they were up and when they were down they were down and when they were half way up they were neither up nor down."

Back in the Long Bar of the Shepheard's Hotel invaluable comment was being passed.

"Bad show all round Billingsworth. Two defeats at Gaza will not go well with the War Office," said Colonel Fotheringham Jones as he finished his third gin and tonic.

"Sack the lot of them I would say. Put someone like you or me in their place. That's what I would say," replied Billingsworth.

"But then who would keep the home fires burning old son?"

"My thoughts exactly! Corporal another refill here. That's a good chap." And the two colonels continued their game of chess in the Long Bar.

Chapter 19: A Welcome Break

Following the Second Gaza battle from April to November 1917 there was no major battle. The British front was five miles south of Gaza and stretched the length of the valley to Beersheba a total of thirty miles. It had to be reinforced and manned so men dug trenches and reinforced the walls with sand bags. Barbed wire was stretched to ensure the patrols would not be surprised suddenly.

From April to September the sun was frying pan hot. Temperatures of 110 degrees Fahrenheit were the usual day temperatures and evening temperatures smouldered in the high nineties. A rest day was still spent maintaining the horses. The railway line now stretched across the Sinai Peninsula coastal road from the Suez Canal 120 miles to within five miles from Gaza.

Low morale resulted in lots of illness. There was an outbreak of mumps, measles and continual colds and flu. Latrines were fly infested so *'Louie the Fly'* was kept busy spreading diseases from latrines to soldiers. The ambulance brigade initiated the building of a rest camp on the beach at Tel el Marakeb. It was five miles west of Wadi Ghuzze along which the troops were encamped. Another recreation camp was established on the cliffs of Khan Yunis about half a mile north of Tel el Marakeb. The Red Cross replenished the camps with books, a piano, chess and lots of other games and low and behold an Australian Rules football.

On the beaches of Gallipoli great battles had been fought and now at Tel el Marakeb a more decisive battle was to be fought. The West Australian troopers against the Victorian troopers! The weapon was Australian Rules football. The battlefield was the sandy oval of Tel el Marakeb beach. The Mediterranean Sea was one boundary the other was the banks of the beach. Seaweed provided other markings. Goal posts were saplings dug into the ground.

Herman led his team onto the field. They wore no tops so were called the West Australian Skins and they opposed the Victorian Shirts. Tom Kendall, a South Australian who knew everything about everything, as all South Australians do, was the umpire. The players took their positions. Eighteen players on each side. The whistle was blown and the ball was thrown up into the air instead of being bounced which was the usual custom. The soft sand did not warrant bouncing.

Herman flew into the air to tap the ball to his rover, Kev Morton who, with the speed of lightning, took off and stab passed the ball to Brendan Duffy waiting in the goals. He took a brilliant chest mark. The crowd roared. Brendan moved back and kicked long and high, scoring a goal. First blood went to the Skins. Some folks consider this an omen that this team would lose but it was not to be. The game was played in good spirit except for the continual punch-ups. Tom Kendal, however, kept reasonable control of the game.

Harry Chauvel on his daily ride watched the game for a short period. Being a Queenslander he was ignorant of the game.

"Thank god they are on my side," he said to his aide de camp and withdrew to his head quarters, which was a mere tent on the banks of the Wadi Ghuzze.

The game ended at sunset with the Skins winning by three clear goals. After match celebrations continued into the night. The match raised the spirits of the boys from the West and increased the determination of the Victorians. It brought wise comments from every other Australian. But all was not so happy on the Russian front.

On March the 8th 1917 the Russian Revolution began. The three hundred year Romanov rule of Russia came to an end. However more significant to the Arab-British relations in the Middle East was the release of the *Picot-Sykes Agreement* which outlined the division of the Ottoman Territories among the Russians, English and French. This was opposed to the *Hussein-McMahon Agreement* which specified the division of the Ottoman territories between the British and Arab nations.

An Imperial War Cabinet Conference was held at 10 Downing Street. Lloyd George, the Prime Minister of England, had decided that the dominions should have more say in the war operations. Up to now all dominions had no say in where troops would be sent. Smuts from South Africa together with Balfour and Robert Cecil strengthened the pro Zionist side and pushed for the capture of the Holy Land and the establishment of a British Colony in Palestine which would then act as a land bridge between India and Egypt bringing together the empires of Africa and Asia.

The war was not going well on the Western Front so what would be more up lifting than the capture of the Holy Land and making it a British colony as if they didn't have enough of these already. The fact that the British were planning to establish a Jewish State within a country that was 90% Arab did not seem to be a problem. Smuts was offered the position to head the army in Egypt because the War Office considered they needed someone a little more flamboyant than Murray. Smuts who was more intent on a political career refused, stating that there were insufficient troops for him to capture Jerusalem. Second choice was Allenby who had failed on the Western Front at Arras. The War Office thought a change of scene might produce better results. So good old Archibald Murray was sacked and replaced by Allenby.

"Allenby I want you to give the British people the Holy Land for Christmas," said Lloyd George the British Prime Minister. Allenby breathed a sigh of relief because he thought he was going to be reprimanded for his inadequacy in Arras.

Lieutenant General Sir Edmund Henry Hyndman Allenby was a tall man who stood at six feet. He had been born in 1861. He was broad shouldered and had a trim sinewy body. His nickname was the 'Bull'. He rode at the front of his men and was meticulous with inspections and even made brigadiers quake with his bull like voice. He was methodical, scholarly and rigid in his ways. Allenby arrived on the 28th of June 1917. He immediately shifted army headquarters from the Shepheard's Hotel in Cairo to Rafa on the Sinai eastern border. "I need to be near the front and I will not have arm chair generals in my army."

"What's the problem Mal?" Maurice Quirke asked when Major Maloney instructed him not to tie his horse to the tree but to hobble it.

"Allenby is making a clean sweep. We are scheduled to extra marches on limited water. No shorts, only long trousers to be worn. I think lads we've got a new leader." Major Maloney informed his men.

"Well what he doesn't see won't hurt him," said Basil Hickey.

"Don't you worry about that! He will be making spot inspections and we'd better measure up."

And spot inspections he made. The warning came. *"Bull Loose"* and Allenby would arrive accompanied by his military secretary, the grandson of Baron Meyer de Rothschild, Lieutenant Colonel Lord Dalmeny, son of the Earl of Roseberry and his Chief of Staff, Brigadier General Archibald Wavell the future Lord Wavell who lost an eye in 1916 and never found it.

The 10th stood pristine, as the Rolls Royce arrived in a flurry of dust. Allenby in full uniform alighted from the car and accompanied by his secretary and head of staff began inspecting the troops. It was Paul Flanagan's fault. He got the giggles and the giggles spread to almost the whole of the 10th.

"What is the matter trooper?" Allenby snapped at trooper Flanagan. "You look bloody funny all dressed up in your egg and bacon accompanied by two pansies dressed up the same. I bet they have never seen a gun," trooper Flanagan remarked respectfully.

Despite the fancy dress they had seen battle and Allenby had lost a son in the Western Front. *"He was considered granite in Europe but in Egypt he turned to steel."* Andrew Barton Paterson wrote in a later journal.

On Paul Flanagan's remark Allenby turned to Dalmeny and remarked, *"Australians are a little strange,"* and moved on undeterred by the derogatory remark.

The Shepheard's Hotel was a little vacant but several regulars kept up the tradition of the British army.

"Your move Billingsworth," said colonel Fotheringham Jones in the Long Bar in the Shepheard's Hotel. They were taking their time to move from the Shepheard's Hotel and after all they had not taken annual leave for some time.

"This Allenby is a bit of a number isn't he?" Billingsworth commented.

"Yes, but well connected. His secretary and Chief of Staff are of royal blood."

"Well so they should be. I must say I found it strange that the Prime Minister consulted with the colonials."

"What can you expect? He leans towards the Zionist you know."

"I didn't know that. Well that explains a lot of things. I think that is checkmate, old chap."

"Damn it old chap that is three in a row. I say who are those gentlemen over there in the bay window."

"I've got no idea old chap. Corporal who are those gentlemen over there in the bay window?"

"They are five colonels, Sir."

"What in dickens name sort of uniform are they wearing?"

"They are undercover agents, Sir. Just dropped in for a cold one."

"Never heard of such a thing. I am going to investigate. Top up my drink please, old chap." He staggered to the table where five officers were seated enjoying a cold beer.

"Excuse me gentlemen but I do not recognise the uniform and this is a Senior Officers' Club."

"I am sorry, Sir. I am colonel Hickey and this is colonel Murphy, Ryan, Quirke and Flanagan. We are undercover agents for Brigadier Allenby. Very hush hush."

"Yes of course, of course, hush hush. Well, carry on gentlemen," he commented and muttered to himself as he returned to his table. "Darnedest thing I've ever heard of."

Hickey and his fellow troopers disguised as officers had been sent to Moascar to collect replacements for the 10th. The replacements were due to arrive in two days time on the 6th August. After their night on the town in Cairo wearing borrowed uniforms from various officers, they returned to Moascar camp by train. On the morning of the 5th they went to the corral where new horses were being broken in. Major Andrew Barton (Banjo) Paterson was looking at a single horse in the corral. Paterson was the senior officer of the remount unit.

"What's his name?" Herman asked.

"Thunder," replied Paterson. "We've been working on this one for several weeks and I must say I am beat. I think we might have to assign him to a Brigadier."

"Go on Murph, you have a go," Quirke sarcastically remarked.

"I'll have a go but you blokes get lost for a while," replied Herman.

"Ok, we'll leave you alone. What about some tea and fresh scones?" suggested Banjo and the group moved off muttering which indicated Flanagan was taking bets.

When the men left, Herman sat on one of the railings and began to whistle a soft Irish ditty his grandfather had taught him. Thunder was black except for his right fore hoof which was white. The horse pricked his ears to the tune.

"You know you're more of a Sock to me than a Thunder," said Herman quietly.

As Herman spoke the stallion stopped rearing and squealing and pig rooting and snorting. Curiosity got the better of him and he came over to Herman and began to sniff. He then reared up and stomped his feet within inches of Herman. Herman was not intimidated and kept on whistling *'Oh Danny Boy'* his favourite Irish ditty. The angry stallion stomped and stomped again. Herman didn't flinch, just kept on whistling. Finally, Herman stood up and stretched, then reached into his pocket and pulled out several lumps of sugar. One he popped into his mouth the others he offered the horse. The horse tentatively took them.

"Some bugger's been belting you haven't they? You have lost trust in men haven't you?" For the next hour the two talked. One in Aussie, the other in horse.

When the men returned, they stood on the corral railings.

"Well Murph how did you go?" asked Banjo.

"We'll see," replied Herman.

"Five quid says you won't last one minute," Quirky encouraged his mate.

"Two quid, he won't last thirty seconds," said Flanagan.

"I reckon you won't even get a saddle on him," said Jackie Ryan.

"Don't need a saddle," said Herman and grabbed the mane and swung onto the horse's back then walked, trotted and cantered around the enclosure.

"Well bugger me," exclaimed Banjo. "How did you do that?"

135

"All in the wrist," replied Herman and both he and the horse grinned.

The men passed over their money to trooper Murphy. "If you don't mind, I would like to give this mount to one of the incoming, Banjo."

"He's all yours mate. But tell us how did you do it?" asked Banjo.

"You wrote, *The Man from Snowy River*. You should know. You simply build up trust. You trust a mate. A horse out here is a mate, not an enemy, not a vehicle. And mates talk to each other. Simple," explained Herman.

"Bloody horse whisperer eh? Come on I'll buy you all a beer," said Banjo and they moved off to the officers' club.

The troopship *Lincoln* arrived at Suez on the 6th of August 1917. The 483 passengers disembarked and felt the land still rocking to the motion of the ocean swell. The replacements for the Light Horse Regiments had cared for the 500 horses during the five-week voyage. Mick Foley was a farmer from Greenough Flats near Geraldton in West Australia. He was six foot one and weighed a wiry eleven stone. His curly black hair mopped his head. He would be twenty-one on the 17th of August. He led his mounts down the landing gangplanks and was met by a group of Light Horsemen.

"G'day mate. My name's Herman Murphy. You are Mick Foley? Right? We have to escort you to Moascar and then to the front. I've got a mount for you to ride back. His name is Socks."

"Thanks Herman," Mick Foley spoke quietly. "This is Barry Clay, Freddie Coombs, Chappy Mc Cormack and Tommy O'Farrell. We are all for the 10th."

All were welcomed and names exchanged. Each told their story as they made the journey to Moascar and then on the train to Wadi

Ghuzze. Herman took both Mick Foley and Socks under his wing. The 10th patrolled the British defences on the Gaza-Beersheba Line regularly.

A slight breeze drifted through the valley that separated the Turkish defences from the British. Herman and his fellow troopers tethered their mounts on the southern side of the redoubt. Herman, Mick Foley, Paul Flanagan and Freddy Coombs relieved Maurice Quirke, Basil Hickey, Barry Clay and Chappy McCormack.

"All quiet on the northern front,' said Maurice Quirke as he stretched his legs and allowed Herman to slip in behind the machine gun. Mick took the feed position from Barry Clay. Paul and Freddy relieved Basil Hickey and Chappy McCormack.

"Johnny Turk is building up his defences on the redoubts over there," said Basil Hickey. "I would say there are over a hundred men in each redoubt." The four men joined with the other members of the patrol and returned to Wadi Ghuzze for a well earned few days rest.

The Turks had used the time from April to August to reinforce their Gaza front. The line of trenches and barbed wire stretched from Gaza to Beersheba, a distance of thirty miles. These were supported with the redoubts behind the trenches.

"You've got Gaza, then Ali Muntar where Samson fought the Philistines, and then there is Tank redoubt, Atawineh, Tel el Sheria and Hareira and Beersheba," Herman pointed out the redoubts on the hills which stretched from Gaza to Beersheba.

"We will rotate two hours at a time. If anything moves, shoot it," Herman explained.

"What were the other two battles for Gaza like, Murph?" Mick Foley asked just to be sociable.

"Simple. The allies lined up here and the Turks lined up there. The British moved in and messed about a bit and then retreated," Herman explained wishing to be quiet. Mick saw that the big Aussie wanted quiet so he settled into his position and let his thoughts run free.

During the night watch, Herman saw movement so opened fire. Next morning a shepherd and all his sheep lay dead. A mistake of war that Herman would have to carry in the recesses of his mind for a very long time. After two days in the redoubt the group was relieved. Mick had had his first taste of the war.

Lawrence, tired of being in the desert and feeling the need for a bath and to be deloused, organised a meeting with Allenby in the Long Bar. He walked into the Bar barefooted and wearing a long silk shirt, Arabic style.

"I say, Corporal, are they allowing Arabs in here now?" asked colonel Billingsworth as Lawrence wafted past his table.

"That is Lieutenant Colonel Thomas Edward Lawrence. He is here to meet with Brigadier Allenby, Sir."

"Well, he certainly wouldn't pass the sock inspection. Could you top up my drink old chap?" Billingsworth commented and returned to his game of chess.

Lawrence wanted money, supplies and arms for the Arab troops he was commanding. Allenby agreed to provide the support Lawrence wanted. Allenby commenced a weeding out process trying one general after the other so that he would get the best of the best. He had planned that the Mounted Division would spear head the attack on Gaza and then on into Jerusalem. Allenby increased the size of the Desert Column and gave the command to Chauvel.

"That Allenby has lost his mind," commented Fotheringham Jones in the Long Bar. "What is he thinking? Fancy giving the command of the largest troop of mounted men to an Australian. Incredible. I am going to suggest a full inquiry."

"But they are mainly Australian Cavalry," replied Billingsworth.

"I suppose you are right. Should never have brought the colonials into this war. That's what I say. A top up please Corporal," added Fotheringham Jones as he buried his head in the *Egyptian Times.*

Allenby planned to break the formidable Gaza line from inland. He would feint an attack on Gaza from the south but would strike east through Beersheba. Beersheba had water; its elaborate wells dated back thousands of years to Abraham. He did not want to disappoint the War Office. He had promised Jerusalem by Christmas and by Christmas he would give them Jerusalem. The ground swell of political thought to capture Jerusalem and establish a Jewish State in Palestine brought Allenby extra aeroplanes, battalions, battleships and over 10,000 cans of asphyxiating gas.

Chapter 20: Beersheba and the Third Battle of Gaza

"Great coats only,' Major Maloney instructed his unit.

"What about tooth brushes?" asked Barry Clay giving a toothless smile. His four front teeth had been knocked out in a fight back in Perth while he was at school. He had a beautiful set of false teeth that made him look quite handsome. He thought himself to be a ladies' man.

"Take your teeth, Clayey. We don't want you spitting over us all day," chirped Freddy Coombs.

The men had to pack all their belongings into their kit bags and turn them into the Q-store.

"You're going on a long ride and you won't be coming back," explained Maloney.

On the 24th of October 1917, the push to Jerusalem commenced. Planes flew continuously over Beersheba and kept the air free of German planes.

On the 27th of October, the British artillery began to bombard Gaza. This was a ruse to trick the Turks into believing the major attack would be through Gaza but Allenby had planned to capture Beersheba in the east and then move west to Gaza.

The men slipped into their saddles on the 28th of October as the sun was setting. They wore their tunic, shirt, underwear, hat, two bandoleers of ninety rounds each, rifle, bayonet and greatcoat strapped to their saddle. Their saddlebags carried toiletries. Freddie Coombs had his packed with dates. He had a sweet tooth. Counting Freddie Coombs there were 100,189 men who took the field in this operation.

The operation consisted of three corps:
The Desert Mounted Corps of 745 officers and 17,935 others.
20th Corps of 1,435 officers and 44,171 others,
21st Corps of 1,154 officers and 34,759 others.

In addition to well over 6,000 horses, 30,000 camels and thousands of mules, there were about 11,600 horses in the Desert Mounted Corps. This included the Anzac Mounted Division of 5,000 cavalrymen and the Australian Mounted Division of 5,000 cavalrymen, and the 7th Mounted Brigade of 1,000 cavalrymen. The Australian Mounted Division included the Third Brigade. The 10th Australian Light Horse Regiment was part of the Third Brigade and was the spearhead. They were often thirty to forty miles ahead of the main infantry unit.

After riding for most of the night, at 2.30 am on the morning of the 29th, the men were given a break at Khalasa, a small town 15 miles southwest of Beersheba. The men unsaddled their horses and gathered around the food wagons and ambulance wagons that waddled behind the cavalry. Breakfast was biscuits and tea. Freddie Coombs had dates with his biscuits. The men then found a comfortable spot and rested. The sun rose and delivered its heat unsympathetically. The men moved to what shade they could find. They rested through the day. Towards evening Major Maloney called his squad in and gave them a small motivation speech.

"Well fellas, it's all or nothing now," said Major Maloney. "We have to take Beersheba and Gaza then push right through to Jerusalem. They want us to be in Jerusalem by Christmas."

"Shit Mal we'll be in Damascus before you can bless yourself," bragged Paul Flanagan, *"Strike and Strike Quickly, that* is our motto.*"*

"I'm on strike right now," said Kev Morton as he pulled his hat over his eyes and went to sleep.

"I'm more afraid of old Allenby than Johnny Turk. So once we start we just keep going. How far is Constantinople from here?" joked Chappy Mc Cormack.

"Let's do it for the lads who went down at Nek," said Herman Murphy on a more serious note. "It's going to be a long ride but this is our grand final." He heard big Bill Fraser's voice in his mind.

"Our task is to go on a wide arc around Beersheba and attack from the northeast. The time for attack is scheduled for five hundred hours on the 31st. Chauvel will give us orders when to mount our attack," Major Maloney explained. The men resaddled their horses. Standing four abreast, the 10th waited for the command.

"Right lads. Forward," Major Maloney directed not wanting his voice to carry across the valley.

"Do you want a cadence, Mal," asked Paul Flanagan.

"No!"

"Shame we have been working on a great version of the Grand Old Duke of York."

"With Allenby it should be something to do with, 'Bull Loose! Bull Loose! Turn back he'll cook your goose!' "quipped Basil Hickey.

"Respect gentleman!" Maloney ordered.

In all 40,000 men were laying siege of Beersheba. The 10th led the Mounted Division. They moved on a wide arc east. They rode 30 miles and by the evening of the 30th of October, they were in position five miles from Tel El Saba, a hill, which rose 1,000 feet on the northeast of Beersheba. The men settled in Wadi Hora. This wadi was connected to the deep Wadi Saba, which ran past Tel el Saba. Here they unrolled their greatcoats and rested. Freddie Coombs ate a couple of dates.

"Hey Mick, you awake?" Herman asked at 4.00 am as the first shaft of light began to frighten the night away.

"Bloody cold Murph."

"We are into winter in this area now." The men woke tied their greatcoats to their saddle, had a drink of water, and then attended to their toiletries.

"I can never get used to wiping my bum with a stick," said Barry Clay.

"You're lucky to find one here," said Jack O Halloran who rarely spoke.

Mick Heathorne got the giggles. The men were ready for the battle that awaited them.

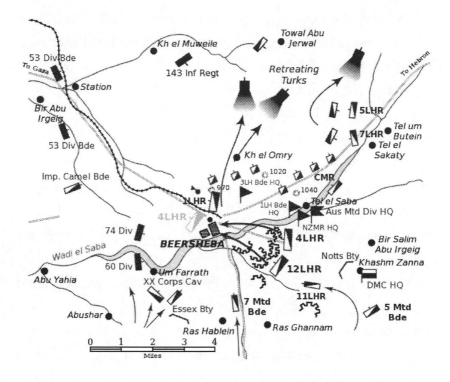

Fig.14. Strategy for the taking of Beersheba

At 5.50 hours Chetwode's artillery commenced firing on Beersheba from the southwest. Their barrage was effective and they moved their cannons to within five miles of the little town.

"Ok lads, it is our job to back up the New Zealanders. It is their job to take Tel el Saba," said Major Maloney. At 10.00 hours the 3rd Anzac Regiment moved along Wadi Hora to 1,000 yards of Tel el Saba. They left their horses and moved under cover of the wadi to within 500 yards and opened fire. Progress was slow because of the steep incline of the bank of the wadi.

At 13.00 the 2nd Anzac Regiment made a gallant mounted charge from the north and came under heavy fire. They immediately retreated, dismounted and counterattacked. The Turks thought the 2nd was retreating so fired at the horses, this gave the 3rd the opportunity to gain ground. Chauvel was not pleased with the delay, so he sent in the 9th and 10th Regiments to assist the Anzac Mounted Regiments. The 10th were 1,000 yards from Tel El Saba. They were dismounted and were resting. Kev Morton lay propped against the bank, his hat over his face snoring peacefully.

"Wake up, Tex," said Herman as he kicked Tex's feet. The young farmer opened his eyes. "Fix bayonets, mate." Like the champion cricketer he was, he became immediately focussed. It was as if the captain had said, *'you're in'*. The 800 men of the 10th led their horses under cover of the wadi to within 300 yards of the foot of Tel El Saba.

"You ready, Mick?" Herman asked Mick Foley.
"Ready as I ever will be," said Mick Foley.
Herman stroked both the neck of his horse, Peter and that of Mick Foley's horse, Socks. "Be back in a minute," he said speaking to his horse. "Look after Socks for me."

They commenced at a jog and then with one almighty roar, charged up the bank and into the enemies' redoubt. Here the Turks were in deep trenches, the walls of which were packed with sand bags. With the agility of a gazelle Tex Morton leapt the sand bags and landed feet away from a Turk. He swung the butt of his rifle into the jaw of the unsuspecting Turk and then drove his bayonet straight through his heart, pulled it out and repeated it on the next man. On his side Herman did the same and Mick did the same until the five remaining Turks lay cowering against the wall of the redoubt with their hands up.

"Hold them," Herman ordered and looked over the edge of the redoubt. Many of the Turks were retreating to the town, returning fire as they went. He called to a couple of Anzacs.

"Keep your eyes on these Johnny Turks, mate. We'll run down the buggers heading for the town," Herman then turned to Tex and Mick. "Come on let's get our horses and run those buggers down."

The rest of the 10th who covered the ground to their horses in seconds rapidly joined them. Herman gave his familiar whistle and Peter trotted to the sound, bringing Socks with him. Herman grabbed the horn of the saddle and leapt into the seat. At full gallop they charged down the wadi and out onto the basin and then into the town. Simultaneously, the thunder of the 4th and the 12th could be heard coming from the southeast.

"Bloody Victorians and South Aussies," said Basil Hickey as he pulled abreast of Herman.

"Two quid says we beat 'em to the town," said Freddie Coombs as he stood in his stirrups, put his head behind his horse's mane and charged jockey style.

"You'll get shot in the arse if you don't sit in the saddle you idiot," cried out Jackie Clare.

The 4th and the 12th had a clear run into the town but not the 9th and 10th. Shrapnel showered them and then a lone German airplane attacked. The Vickers machine gun from the plane shot death into the 10th. Mick Heathorne fell. He was dead before he hit the ground. He lay there with a smile on his face. His stomach had been shot away. Barry Clay with his teeth safely tucked in his saddlebag spat a curse. "Bastards!" he spurred on his horse.

Shrapnel took off the top of Chappy Mc Cormack's head. The plane dropped its remaining bombs. It blew a hole in the charging 10th. Herman's tunic ripped as pieces of shrapnel took up residence in his arm. He only felt a slight mosquito bit of pain and kept riding. He leant over his mounts ear. "If we get this town Peter we will have a long drink."

Fig 15. Beersheba 1917

147

Fig 16. Charge into Beersheba

Fig.17. On the gallop into Beersheba

Fig. 18. Beersheba gained.

They hit the first trenches and leapt them, then pulled rein, dismounted and jumped into the trenches. Tex Morton was already into action. It appeared as if he was batting to make a century in a cricket match. With the precision of an opening batsman, he took on man after man. The rifle butt hit the chin of the Turk. Crack! The bayonet entered the body. There was a scream of pain and then he moved to the next. Herman was beside him as was Mick. The trench empty, they rode into the city.

The 4th had beaten them to the centre of the town. The wires to blow up the wells had been cut. The town was taken. The 10th gathered near the mosque in the centre of the town. Tex found a well, filled his hat with water and watered his horse then found a wall, slid down it and went to sleep. After attending to their horses, Herman, Mick, Jackie Clare and Maurice Quirke went scrounging for food. They returned to the homing signal of Tex Morton's snoring, built a fire and roasted a goat, several chickens and a sheep. As the succulent meats were roasting, they squatted and had a cup of billy tea, thanks to the faithful food wagons, which had never deserted their men.

"An Aussie soldier marches on his billy tea," remarked Fremantle Freddie, a tall wharfie from Fremantle.

Spirits were high in the camp that night. Even the horses had a couple of horselaughs among themselves.

Chapter 21: Taking Jerusalem

On the day after the capture of Beersheba, the British 7th Mounted Brigade (with the Australian 8th Light Horse Regiment attached) raced to Khuweilfe to try to take it before the Turks strengthened the position, but they arrived too late. Tel el Khuweilfeh was a dominating hill ten miles to the north of Beersheba: it also had an excellent water supply. Here the Turks launched a counterattack. For the next four days, the British, Australian and New Zealand mounted brigades attempted to capture the Khuweilfe position. Each night a brigade would be relieved in order to return its horses to the water at Beersheba and another brigade would resume the assault.

"How did you go?" asked a trooper from the 4th as they relieved the 10th.

"I shot two sticks, three rocks, one lizard and I think I put a hole through a Turk's hat," replied Paul Flanagan who climbed into his saddle and returned to Beersheba with his mates. Here they watered and groomed their horses and then slept. Tex Morton was asleep as soon as he hit the saddle.

"There seems to be more Turks every time we face those trenches," Basil Hickey remarked on the return.

"We'll have to break through soon or we'll have the whole Turkish army up there," Herman added. At dawn on the 6th of November, a concerted effort was made to take Tel el Khuweilfeh.

"Why don't we just charge up the hill and take the bloody trenches?" asked Jackie Ryan who had become frustrated with the way the battle was going.

"Because you would get no more than a few yards and those machine guns would riddle you with bullets and that hurt," said Herman. In response to Jackie's frustration the cannons of the Light Horse Artillery opened up and began a series of nonstop blasts.

"That's put the shit up 'em," said Jackie Clare.

"Fix bayonets," called Major Maloney.

"Bugger off, Mal. It's half a mile to those trenches. I'm not running all that way on an empty stomach," complained Freddie Coombs whose supply of dates had run out.

"Those Irish and English yeomen are making a charge. I thought you might like to join them," remarked Major Maloney.

"Bayonet fixed, major," responded Freddie determined not to be out done by any *pommy bastard"*. With a scream that would have wakened the dead, the 10th charged up the hill to the Turk's trenches. Bullets ripped through Freddie's' stomach showing it wasn't empty after all. A single shot hit Bernie Ring right between the eyes. He died immediately. This infuriated the men as they ran faster and leapt into the trenches showing no mercy. Back to back, Herman and Mick Foley fought. Kev Morton once again was batting for a century. The Turks withdrew. The 10th returned to their horses to give chase. But the ground was too rough and the horses too dry for a successful follow up. Tel el Khuweilfeh had been taken with its ready supply of water. The men spent the night in Tel el Khuweilfeh. Around the campfire they reflected on the day.

"Freddie would have liked these dates," said Paul Flanagan and all were silent.

Next morning news came through that Gaza had been taken.

"That means those *pommy bastards* can go all the way to Jerusalem along the coast," said Maurice Quirke.

"Nothing like a battle with an ocean view," cracked Mick Foley.

"Ok lads let's push on," said Major Maloney on the 8th of November.

The final score for this round was:

British: 18,000 killed wounded or missing

Turks: 25,000 losses including 12,000 prisoners.

From Beersheba to Jerusalem it was forty-five miles. Jerusalem was forty miles inland from the sea. From Beersheba to Jerusalem the land was compacted yellow ochre shale that sometimes reached to hills of a thousand feet high and gorges a thousand feet deep. It was shade less, waterless and ruthless. Here goats ate sticks and Bedouins ate goats. Occasionally there was an oasis and the oasis had water, which made them priceless when fighting a war, as the major vehicle was a horse, donkey or camel. They moved east towards Huj and al Jemmamah. Here they met over 5000 Turkish troops dug in and with cannon support. There were only five hundred horsemen who stopped the counterattack.

"I could grow to like those Turks," said Basil Hickey, "but every time we meet them they shoot at us. What have they got against us?"

"We are trying to take their country," said Herman as he fired several rounds for effect.

"Give me a home among the gum trees,
With lots of plum trees,

With a sheep or two
And a kangaroo
And clothes line at the back
And a veranda in the front
And my old rocking chair,"

Paul Flanagan could not resist an opportunity to break into song.

All day the five hundred kept the Turks at bay. On the 9th of November they were joined by the 3rd, 9th, 8th, 5th and the 7th. With increased numbers the Turks began to withdraw.

"They're withdrawing the cannons," said Jackie Clare as he observed the Turks bring up a bullock team to withdraw the cannon. "I reckon we could take those cannon."

"Go for it," said Major Maloney. "I'll join you."

"We'll take the cannon on the left," the major said referring to Jack Clare, Herman Murphy and Mick Foley, Jack Ryan and Maurice Quirke. "Brendan, you, Paul, Tex and Barry Clay take the one to the right. Remo, you, Jack O'Halloran, Tommy O' Farrell and Dutchy Holland take that one near that small rise." Dutchy was a new recruit who had joined the group in the last couple of days. He was dark and of medium build and came from a sheep farm around Dongara in West Australia.

"Wait for my order," said Major Maloney. When the teams of shaggy Turkish bullocks were being harnessed to the cannon the order was given. The men charged at full gallop towards the cannon. Taken by surprise the Turks fired at the charging Aussies. The Aussies covered the ground in record time. Herman slid from his saddle and whacked a Turk under the chin. The Turk fell to the ground. A German officer who was in charge of the cannon crew saw the wisdom of surrender.

In clear English he said. "I am a German officer and I demand the respect due to a German officer." He stood arrogantly eyeing the Aussies up and down.

"Bugger you," said Jacky Ryan and whacked him under the chin with the butt of his rifle putting the officer to sleep.

"Round up the bullocks, Murph, and harness them to the cannon," Maloney ordered.

"These cattle don't understand English," Herman replied as the bullocks were going everywhere.

"Well shot 'em," ordered Maloney and they did.

Some six hundred prisoners were taken together with four cannon.

"They'll make a nice decoration in some park for the kids to play on," said Jack Ryan and sat down and rolled himself a smoke.

The Turks withdrew to high ground. The ridge ran from the villages of Katrah to El Mughar. The ridge was surrounded by hilly terrain, here the main north south railway line met at Second Station. Allenby's troops moved along the Gaza-Jerusalem road on the west and the Mounted Division was dispersed on the east. On the 13th of November, the 10th were looking across 3,000 yards of shot-covered ground to the trenches of El Mughar.

"We go at 7.00 am," Major Maloney told his men who were resting in Wadi Jamus, which ran at right angles to the ridge.

"I'm taking the day off, Mal. Thirteen is an unlucky number," said Paul Flanagan.

"Unlucky for some lucky for others" said Mick Foley. "That is the number of my footy jumper."

"What? Did Greenough ever win? I think you had the wooden spoon ten years in a row," said Herman.

At 7.00 am all hell broke loose. Cannons, machine guns, rifle fire all opened up. The 10th remained in reserve. At 2.00 pm the 6th Mounted Brigade made an open charge towards the ridge.

"What the bloody hell are those poms doing?" Maloney asked.

"I think they are charging the ridge, Mal," said Basil Hickey.

"Mount up men. They'll be cut to pieces."

The Mounted Brigade consisting of 800 English and Irish Yeoman, charged on horse across the 3,000 yards of the plain, dismounted, and then did a full bayonet charge up the ridge.

"What the hell do you think you're doing paddy," Jackie Ryan asked as he ran beside an Irishman.

"Tis a good day for it to be sure to be sure," was the reply.

The Ridge was secured. The battle continued until Second Station was secured and the troops didn't stop. They pushed on taking Ramleh and Ludd on the railway line north, and advanced east to Latron. The railway was secured which cut off one line of supply to the Turks. In the week's fighting since taking Beersheba some 1,400 Turkish troops had been lost while the British had lost 616.

The Mounted Division moved north and on the 15th of November the 10th moved into Jaffa. Jaffa was the old port through which Herod had brought the cedars from Lebanon to build his palace. This was the port where the ancient Phoenicians ventured into the unknown world to ply their trade. This was a thriving city that the weary troops had to organize.

Fig. 19. 10th Rounding up prisoners in Jaffa, 15th November 1917

As the 10th rode their horses through the city, they were a motley sight, children hid behind their mother's skirts, old men squinted, and few smiled.

"This looks just like Fremantle," said Jack O'Hallaron.

"Sure does," replied Basil Hickey. "It is a wharf filled with wharfies."

"And the best footballers in the West," O'Hallaron added.

"Rubbish," replied Herman Murphy. "You Dockers have no idea about footy."

"Looky here," said Maurice Quirke as he sighted the Park Hotel. "I think there are conspirators in here."

He pulled rein and slid off his saddle. He was joined by Jackie Ryan, Jackie Clare, Herman Murphy and Mick Foley.

"Paul, mind the horses. These wogs would steal them if you left them unguarded." commanded Jackie Ryan, assuming an air of importance.

"Don't be long," replied Paul. "Then it is my turn."

As the dishevelled troopers entered the ornate hotel, the sycophant manager greeted them. "Welcome to the Park Hotel, Gentleman. We are great supporters of the British soldier."

"We are Aussies and you can take the German Flag down and show us the best room in the hotel," said Jack Clare.

"The flag! A mere oversight. The best room was occupied by the owner, gentleman, Baron Ustinov. He is a pilot in the German army but he had to leave on urgent business." The Baron's room was luxury personified. He was after all the grandfather of renowned movie star Peter Ustinov.

"These Germans know how to fight a war. What do you think lads?" asked Maurice Quirke, evaluating the luxurious surrounds. It was tempting but he was in a fighting mood and wanted to complete his mission. *'Jerusalem by Christmas,'* was his thought. Herman verbalized his thinking.

"To be honest I want to rest when it's over. Not now," said Herman Murphy, and the lads agreed to leave the Park Hotel and move on.

"What do you mean they had no beer?" Paul Flanagan asked as the 10th headed east to Jerusalem.

Several regiments of the Mounted Division took occupation of the city. Gangs of sweepers were employed and the city was swept clean. The New Zealanders took charge of the sole Hospital. Jerusalem was in the sights of the 10th. They kept moving. Both the 7th Turkish army under Fevasi Pasha and the 8th Army under Kress von Kressenstein drew back to defend Jerusalem. On the 18th of November Allenby directed his army to move towards Jerusalem.

And then the rain came. It came in buckets. It turned every wadi into a river, every gorge into a lake and every slope into a mud slide.

Horses and cannon sank into the compacted shale. The sandy loam turned to mud. Horses sank so far they broke their legs. The men had no protection from the wet or the cold as their greatcoats and clothing were not waterproof. At night they took cover by climbing into a hole or leaning against an ancient wall with a cup of billy tea, and if lucky, a tin of bully beef. There was no real front just sniping and swearing at the weather. Conditions were so bad that in the last two months of 1917, 10,000 horses, camels, mules and donkeys became casualties and most eventually died.

Only one regiment, the 10th Light Horse Regiment represented Australia in the final attack on Jerusalem. As they pushed through to Jerusalem, the muddy paths were strewn with dead Turkish soldiers and animals, which provided a delightful feast for jackals at night and crows in the day. On the 24th of November conditions became so bad Allenby called a halt.

"What do you mean halt?" said Major Maloney to the signaller. "This is a bog hole. We are going to high ground. You will find us in Bethlehem."

"*Percute et Percute Velocitor*. Strike and strike swiftly is our motto," added the officer.

"What?" asked the signaller who did not quite understand the Latin motto.

"You beauty! You bloody beauty," explained Jackie Ryan whose Latin was a little astray.

Bethlehem is about eight miles south of Jerusalem. It sits snugly in the Judean hills, which overlook Jerusalem and rise 2,000 feet above sea level. Falkenhayn was in charge of the Turkish army. He had withdrawn both the 7th and 8th armies to defend Jerusalem and he was awaiting reinforcements but the British, however, had captured the north-south railway line from Constantinople, so his supply had to come from Hejaz or Amman. Lawrence and his rebel Arabs were constantly invading the Hejaz line. Consequently he was short on reserves. When the rain eventually stopped, Allenby sent Chetwode with the 20th Division to attack Jerusalem from the west. The Mounted Division on the other hand moved in from the southeast.

On the 7th of December it was cold and wintry. The temperature at midday was a very chill fifty degrees Fahrenheit. The 10th looked down on Bethlehem. The stark, white flat-topped houses contrasted with the soggy yellow ochre shale. Green trees and new grass looked enticing. There were still a few puddles of water here and there. Some 900 trenches zig-zagged around the southern border of the town. Here Turkish soldiers stood in inches of mud and slosh. Some had the odd sand bag or two to sit on.

"Where's the stable Jesus was born in?" Dutchy Holland asked.

"See that white house on the left hand side of the road," said Basil Hickey.

"Yes," responded Dutchy.

"Just behind there."

"Oh," said the enlightened Dutchy, not knowing that a rather large church marked the position of the original stable.

"Last road into Jerusalem. Both the British and the Turks have agreed not to fight in the city of Jerusalem. So this is our last battle before Jerusalem," Major Maloney explained.

"Let's do it then," said Jackie Clare flicking away his butt and pulling back on his machine gun.

All along the Judean hills the machine guns barked and spat their death into the trenches below. The land was not suited to a cavalry charge, so the men fired, moved forward and fired again. The horses sat quietly in the background and talked among themselves. Within five hundred yards, the men fixed bayonets and with one mighty roar, charged forward, slipping and sliding as they went. They leapt the embankments of the trenches. The trenches were empty. The Turks had withdrawn leaving Jerusalem to the British.

"That was easy," said Dutchy Holland.

"It's your squeaky voice that does it," said Basil Hickey.

"Back in the saddle men," ordered Major Maloney. "We are off to Jerusalem."

"I thought you said there was to be no fighting around Jerusalem, Mal," said Paul Flanagan.

"Never trust an officer and never trust the enemy," came the reply.

The men fell in behind Maloney, Herman Murphy with Mick Foley, then Maurice Quirke and Jack Ryan, Jackie Clare with Barry Clay, Paul Flanagan with Dutchy Holland, Basil Hickey and Remo Genetti, Brendan Duffy and Jack O'Hallaron, then came Tex Morton followed by the rest of the 10th.

"A cadence trooper," called Maloney. Paul Flanagan began:

"Bring the good ol' Bugle boys! We'll sing another song,
Sing it with a spirit that will start the world along,
Sing it like we used to sing it fifty thousand strong,
While we were marching through Georgia."

The men joined in:

"Hurrah! Hurrah! We bring the Jubilee,
Hurrah! Hurrah! The flag that makes you free,
So we sang the chorus from Atlanta to the sea,
While we were marching through Georgia."

The Mounted Division pulled rein on the outskirt of the city of Jerusalem. They dismounted and settled under the protection of a ridge. All slept the fitful sleep of men during battle. On the following morning Paul Flanagan stretched his legs and his feet stuck out from under his greatcoat.

"Hey, Murph, I will have eggs and bacon for breakfast," Paul joked.

"Why not," responded Herman and kicked his greatcoat off. "Any one wants to come and collect the eggs?"

"Yeah I'll come."

"Me too."

So Herman, Maurice Quirke and Jack Clare wandered tentatively over the small rise hoping to see a small farm with some eggs. They carried their rifles with them. Seeing that all was clear, they began to descend towards a small farmhouse. When they reached the farmhouse, they saw a small redoubt with four Turkish soldiers holding up a white flag.

"You go and talk to them Murph, you can speak their language. We will cover you," directed Maurice Quirke.

Herman moved to the soldiers. Words were exchanged and he returned.

"What did they say?" asked Jack Clare.

"It's for the major's ears only."

They collected eggs on the way back to the men.

"Major, I have serious news for you. The Turks have left Jerusalem because they didn't want to hear our singing again."

"Serious?" Maloney asked.

"Dead serious," said Herman.

"Mount up men, we'll breakfast in Jerusalem," said Major Maloney.

The small squadron of men entered the Holy City through the Jaffa Gates. Early morning citizens looked suspiciously at the mounted

Australians. After several hours they rejoined their regiment. Chauvel sent for Major Maloney.

When he returned to his loyal men, he said, "We are in deep shit. Allenby wanted to be the first to enter. His directive issued on the 6th of December and I quote, *'Entering Jerusalem: during the forthcoming operations no officer or troops are to go beyond the outskirts of Jerusalem into the town except in the case of urgent tactical necessity. '"*

"Breakfast is an extreme tactical necessity," explained Herman.

Fig. 20. Allenby Enters Jerusalem 11th December, 1917

Despite their transgression, the 10th Regiment was the only Australian Light Horse Regiment that stood guard outside the Jaffa gates, as Allenby and his entourage entered the city on foot, out of respect for the Holy City. Allenby immediately placed Jerusalem under martial law. He posted guards on all Christian, Muslim and Jewish sacred shrines both in Jerusalem and Bethlehem.

The rain continued to fall. Bridges were swept away. Some soldiers had fallen into mud holes and drowned. Every ditch, gorge and riverbed flowed a torrent. Camels lay down in the water and died. A raging storm struck Jerusalem and its surrounds on Christmas Eve and Christmas Day in 1917, but despite this, the men of the 10th gathered around the shrine of the original stable of Bethlehem and attended a joint service delivered by the Catholic Priest and the Anglican Parson. The men sang the carols with sentiment.

Allenby's army was bogged down around Jerusalem. Some sat in the open and just soaked up the rain and cold. The animals drooped and sank, motionless, in the mud. Herman and his mates had managed to get themselves lodgings with the residents of Bethlehem. Their horses were under makeshift cover. Both man and beast enjoyed the rest as they looked at the grey world through a curtain of water flowing freely off the roof of the flat-topped farmhouse.

"In the last sixty days I've ridden 1,000 miles, drank 200 pannikins of tea, eaten 250 bush biscuits and 30 tins of bully beef, fired 1,500 rounds of ammunition and am still alive," declared Paul Flanagan through an opening in his greatcoat as he sat around the open fire in the farm house. No one challenged the philosophical statement. Tex Morton merely applauded with a snore. The rest sat in sombre silence.

The Turks attempted to retake Jerusalem on the 25th of December but it was a half-hearted affair, hampered by the rain. Blue skies came with the New Year. The horses were ready for exercise. Allenby consolidated his front and then planned to extend his line along the Jordan River, take Jericho and the eastern shores of the Dead Sea. During January the men visited the sacred shrines in and around Jerusalem. Herman bought Iris a pair of rosary beads. The beads were seeds of olives from the Garden of Olives where Jesus prayed before the Roman soldiers took him to be tried and crucified.

Chapter 22: Into the Jordan Valley

"Cadence trooper," called Major Maloney on the 19th of February as the 10th led the Mounted Division towards the Jordan Valley.

"Joshua fit the battle of Jericho, Jericho, Jericho,
Joshua fit the battle of Jericho
And the rains came tumbling down," Paul Flanagan commenced.

"Jocularity will not be part of this man's army. If you want a transfer, Trooper, I am willing to oblige. Despite the inclement weather give us the usual cadence. It might inspire the men," ordered Maloney in serious tones but with a smile on the inside. "It's bloody pissing down Mal," Paul replied. "Trooper Hickey, a cadence," commanded Major Maloney. Hickey commenced, singing the well-known Australian ballad:

"Once a Jolly Swagman camped by a billabong,
Under the shade of a coolabah tree,"

Maloney didn't object even though he thought the Dead Sea was a bit bigger than the average billabong and was a great deal saltier. The men joined in with zest, singing the unofficial Aussie National Anthem, *Waltzing Matilda*. The lyrics had been written by Banjo Paterson to commemorate a shearer's strike in Winton Queensland, 1895. The melody had been taken from a Celtic folk tune, *'Thou Bonnie Wood of Criagielea.'*

Soner Bantun sat in his shallow foxhole, which he had scraped with his four companions a week ago. They were a mile from Jericho on a small embankment that guarded the road to this Holy City. Because the foxhole was on a slope it was well drained. They had placed rocks on the floor to keep it dry. He watched the horsemen negotiating the perilous road that serpented into Jericho. They looked like ants coming for sugar slowly but methodically. He was a farmer's son. Their farm was on the Canakkale Peninsula, which with the Gallipoli Peninsula guarded the Dardanelles. The Dardanelles was a mile wide channel that opened into the inland Marmar Sea, which led to the Black Sea thus giving access to Russia and Central Asia and the Middle East. His farm was a mere forty acres but it provided sufficient lemons, oranges, olives and vegetables to keep him, his father, his mother and his younger sister in food and clothes.

He had joined the Turkish Army at fifteen and had watched the British ships sink in the treacherous straits as they tried to penetrate the inland sea. He remembered the cannon fire from Canakkale and the exploding mines that sank five British and two French ships. He was one of the 160 soldiers who watched the Anzacs land at Anzac Cove. He and his companions had fired on the invaders but when they saw the number of invading troops, they had run only to be met by Mustafa Kemal who said, *'Don't fight for your country die for your country.'* He had returned to his post and had fought through the eight months of horror in Gallipoli. Now he was here and he was cold but the tea was hot. Four years he had been fighting these people who wanted to take over his country.

"Why do they invade my country? Don't they have a country of their own?" His farm was not far from the city of Troy. This city had known many invasions. "Maybe our country has something other countries do not have," he thought.

When the Mounted Division was in range, Soner with the other machine gunners opened fire. He watched the ants disperse, taking cover on the slopes. Within an hour the British Artillery returned fire from a distance of three miles. Soner knew that the Australians would move closer and closer, but there was no danger of a bayonet charge or a cavalry charge. The road was on a ridge and there were no open plains.

The artillery stopped. Machine gun fire commenced. Tufts of sodden mud sprang up into the air. There was so much noise that he didn't even hear the cries of his companions as bullets ripped through their tunics and flesh. They fell into the foxholes still and dead. Their ambitions and plans and laughter stopped there.

He slipped out of his hole and joined others of the advanced patrol who were retreating to the city.

On the morning of February 21st, it was apparent that the Turkish line had been broken, and the Allied forces entered the Holy City of Jericho without much resistance at just after 8 a.m.

Soner was there to watch the horsemen ride through the city. He sat with his back to a wall and smoked an Australian *rolly* and watched these men with the strange hats decorated with feathers.

"They are no different from me," he thought. He was one of the forty-six Turkish soldiers taken prisoner during the battle of Jericho.

The capture of Jericho proved to be an important strategic victory for the Allies, who now controlled some of the most important roads in the region, including the main road to the coast and the mountain highway leading to Jerusalem. They had reached the northern end of the Dead Sea, the lowest point on earth at 1,300 feet below sea level. Allenby from his headquarters in Jerusalem gave orders for all troops to withdraw from the Jordan, except the 10th, which he left to patrol the area. He used the time from the end of February to the beginning of May to reinforce his front, which extended from Jaffa on the west to the Jordan on the east.

The Jordan River is 156 miles long. It begins from the over flow of the Sea of Galilee and travels 156 miles to the Dead Sea. The Sea of Galilee is fed by the tributaries: Hasbani from Lebanon, Banias rising from a spring at the foot of Mt Hermon in the Syrian Ranges, the Dan whose source is also the foot of Mt Hermon, and the Iyon from the Lebanon ranges. The river is virtually a short watercourse that over the years has filled up the Jordan rift. The Dead Sea is so called because it is too salty to sustain any life.

The men of the 10th had built their tent city about a mile north of the Dead Sea. There were fields each side of the Jordan that extended for several miles before rising to shale embankments negotiable only by treacherous winding paths large enough for a mule and a cart. Each morning the troopers would groom their horses and then ride patrol along the banks of the Jordan as far the outskirts of Jericho. Further than this was Turkish territory. As the winter rains subsided, the spring flow of the Jordan began to steady.

"Major, we could build a weir across the Jordan River and flood the river plains and grow some oats for our horses," Herman Murphy suggested. So the men began to build their weir using the rocks from the hillsides.

"Hey Murph, you read the Bible don't you?" asked Paul Flanagan.

"Pretty much," Herman replied.

"Isn't this land the Promised land?"

"I believe it is," Herman agreed.

"I guess the Lord hadn't seen West Australia, eh?" said Barry Clay irreligiously.

"Too far for Moses to walk," added Mick Foley.

"Come to think of it," said Tex Morton waking from his nap, "we have ridden the path Mary and Joseph travelled. Only we have done it backwards. They started in Bethlehem fled to Egypt, then walked back to Nazareth."

"They were pretty tough back into those days," added Dutchy Holland.

On the 15th of April, 1918, as the men of the 10th were gathered around their morning campfires enjoying their mug of billy tea, the order came that they had to attack Es Salt, a town on the west side of the Jordan river some 2,490 feet above sea level. This hillside town was on the main track from the west to Jerusalem. Slowly the Mounted Divisions made their way from their bivouac around Jerusalem, Bethlehem and Jericho. A pontoon bridge had been constructed across the Jordan. As usual the 10th spearheaded the attack. On the 29th they moved across the bridge up the slopes and into the town of Es Salt.

"The Three Wise Men would have travelled along this track," commented Paul Flanagan as the 10th made its way along the paths to Es Salt.

"That proves they were not very wise," said Jack Clare. "This would be the worst road we've ever travelled on."

It was hot but the Mounted Division had moved so rapidly they took the town by surprise. It surrendered quickly but then like a child's game of cowboys and Indians, the Turkish troops attacked the bridge sites and the order was given for the Mounted Division to withdraw, even before Allenby was aware the town had been taken.

Under heavy fire, the troops withdrew. Allenby realized this was not the path that would be taken to advance on Damascus. The 10th was left to patrol the Jordan once again.

"A bloody mess that was," complained Maurice Quirke." Next time we will go a little slower." He took the saddle off his horse and gave his horse a rub down.

Paul hummed to himself,

"The grand old Duke of York, He had ten thousand men, He marched them to the top of the hill then marched them down again."

Tex threw a boot at Paul because the singing was disturbing his sleeping time.

"We need faster pigeons to carry messages. Then Allenby would know what we are doing," Dutchy commented wisely.

"The less he knows the better," Jack Ryan added.

"There are two wise men, you must be the third eh, Murph," Paul wisely philosophised.

Herman merely grunted.

Chapter 23: Battle of Megiddo

The Battle of Megiddo was divided into two sections: the battle in Sharon Plain, which stretches along the coast from Jaffa to the Mount Carmel range and the second battle was in Nabulus, a strategic town in the Judaean Hills which border the Plain of Sharon.

The British War Office because of Megiddo's historical significance chose the name, *Battle of Megiddo.* It was also a nice name for a battle. Once again the leather seated set of the War Office in Britain liked to have things nice and tidy. But the Battle of Megiddo did not take place at Mt Megiddo, which is on the Mount Carmel Ridge. From the top of Mount Megiddo, the Plain of Sharon is a patchwork of green and deep brown fertile soil, which stretches for fifty-six miles from Jaffa in the south, to Mount Carmel in the north. Since 7000 BC Megiddo has been a junction for international traffic. Here more bloody battles have been fought than in any other part of the world. The Bible suggests that this where the final battle will be fought between good and evil. This is the site of Armageddon. Megiddo also overlooks the valley of Jezreel, which is a pass from the Mediterranean Sea through to the Jordan Valley. Several million years earlier, the Mediterranean Sea flowed over the Esdraelon plain through the valley of Jezreel and into the Jordan.

Following the capture of Jerusalem, over half of Allenby's troops were shipped off to support the Western Front. His whole tank division had been moved. When the Turks withdrew from Jerusalem, they created a defence line from the coast on the west to Amman in the east. This line was some twenty miles north of Jerusalem. Eric van Falkenhayn, who was head of the Turkish army, had wanted to withdraw from this area but he was replaced by Otto Liman von Sanders who had his army dig in. Von Sanders argued that retreating was not good for the morale of his men. He set up his head quarters in the town of Nazareth, which was a small town in the hills north of the Esdraelon Plain and directly opposite the Musmus Pass, which stretches fourteen miles through the Mt Carmel Hills. On the other hand, Mustafa Kemal, the Turkish leader of Gallipoli, had set up his headquarters in Nabulus.

During the months of July and August, Allenby's forces were brought up to strength. The men were from India and, although excellent horsemen, could not speak Arabic nor English. They spoke Urdu or Hindustani and none of the allied forces could speak these languages. Despite their inability to speak English, the Indians were ready for battle in a couple of months. Much of this was due to Lieutenant General George Barrow, a former Indian Cavalry Officer. He was placed in charge of the Indian 5th and 4th Divisions.

To pass the time during these months, the 10th Light Horse regiment, which was on permanent patrol in the Jordan Valley, together with the Anzac Mounted Rifles, constructed a dam across the Jordan River and organized several race meetings as well as build a bridge across the Jordan. Each day, however, the Turks sent several rounds of artillery fire into the valley. *Jericho Jenny* as one of the cannons was lovingly called, sent her message daily. In addition to cannon fire, rifle and machine gun fire from the mountain ridges ensured that the Aussies were always on the alert. Worse than the Turks, however, were the mosquitoes. These pests carried all kinds of diseases, including malaria. These little beasties and the heat in the valley, which rose to 120 degrees Fahrenheit, made the Jordan Valley no Promised Land.

Daily the Australian Flying Air Corps flew over the valley and engaged the German Air Corps in aerial acrobatics with bullets. One of the outstanding pilots at this time was Ross Smith who came from Adelaide in South Australia and later made history with his brother Keith Smith by flying from England to Australia in record time.

Allenby's plan was to trick the Turks into believing he would launch a major attack through the east of the Jordan. To convince the Turks he was building up his forces in the valley, he had the 10th quietly ride to the top of the mountains on the side of the Jordan by night and by day ride into the valley dragging brush behind them to cause huge clouds of dust. With this ploy he hoped to convince the Turks that a large number of troops were assembling in the valley.

Mock tents and over 15,000 soldiers and horses, made of wood, were placed in the valley. It was essential that the Turks were kept out of the valley so they would not discover the subterfuge. Yet another Trojan horse was in action to trick the Turks.

When the heat and mosquitoes became overpowering, the men in the Jordan Valley were moved to the ancient reservoirs of Solomon on the road to Beersheba. Here they poured kerosene on the drainage holes to kill mosquitoes and cleared the area of stagnant pools. Once this was done, they were able to enjoy the cooler climate in comfort.

Horses are easier to spot than men. The German Air Force continued to target the horses and made daily runs through the valley dropping bombs and strafing the tents. On the 10th of July the men were moved to Talaat el Dumm, this area is near the wilderness where Jesus spent the forty days and forty nights struggling with the devil. The area gave them protection from the Germans but not the mosquitoes, lice, ticks and sand flies. Then there was always the dust, which got into everything. Swimming in the salty Dead Sea was always a relief for the men.

On the 21st of August 1918 the 10th were moved to Ludd, twenty miles southeast of Jaffa. Here they set up tents under the olive trees and orange trees. But to ensure the Turks did not see them, they were confined to quarters during the day. This gave them the opportunity to play cards and sleep. The officers lectured the men on the dangers of venereal diseases. A very valuable lecture since there was over 20,000 men in Ludd but no women. To ensure that none of the 10th had this disease they were given a delousing bath very much like the way they used *Cooper's Dip* back home on the farm to delouse their sheep. Their clothes were steamed to get rid of the lice. Such enjoyable activities kept the men busy during their camp confinement. Tex Morton, however, slept.

The Anzac Mounted Rifles under General Chaytor remained in the Jordan Valley. He with Lawrence, who was roaming the deserts with the Arabs a little further east, formed the right flank of Allenby's final assault. On September 17th, Arabs under T. E. Lawrence and Nuri As Said began to move north towards Damascus along the Hejaz railway lines, which ran from Mecca to Constantinople. Their first target was the vital rail centre of Deraa. Lawrence's initial forces were a Camel Corps unit from Feisal's Army, an Egyptian Camel Corps unit, some Gurkha machine gunners, British and Australian armoured cars and French mountain artillery. Rualla and Howeitat tribesmen and local insurgents soon joined them.

The Royal Allied Air Force began air raids on Deraa, which added more evidence to the sham that the major attack was through the east. Lawrence was a mere hundred miles to the east of Allenby. The Australian Flying Corps gave him assistance and with the use of carrier pigeons ensured that accurate communication between headquarters and the east flank was maintained. As the Turks reacted to the attacks on Deraa, the units of Chaytor's Corps made attacks in the hills above the Jordan River, further diverting the Turks' attention to the east flank. At the last minute, an Indian deserter warned the Turks about the impending main attack, but he was not believed.

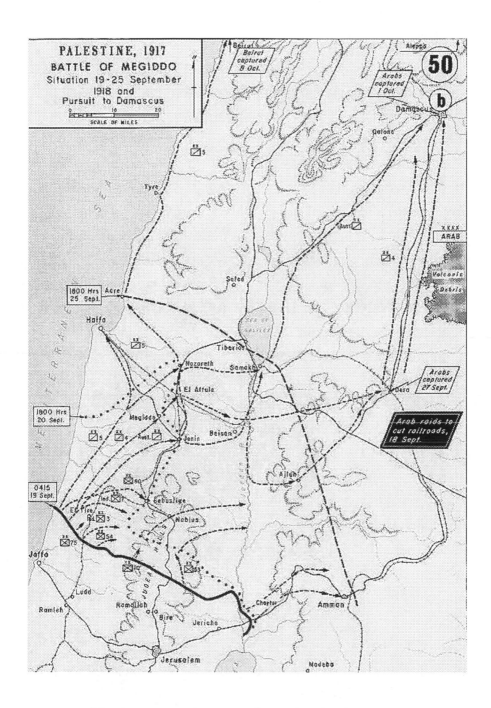

Fig. 21. Battle Megiddo 19ᵗʰ to 25ᵗʰ September, 1918

At 4.30 am on September 19th, Allenby's main attack began. A barrage by 385 guns opened fire on the trenches of the Turks in the Plain of Sharon. The Australian Flying Corps bombed and strafed the entrenchments on the Plain of Sharon. There were two lines of Turkish trenches, which traversed the plain on a five-mile front. The first line was protected with barbed wire and virtually stretched from the sand dunes on the coast to the Judean foothills. The second row of trenches was some three miles behind the first. This line was not protected by barbed wire and was not a continuous line but a series of trenches stretching from the coast to the Judean foothills. Chetwode and his infantry moved into the Judaean Hills. Their target was Nabulus where Mustafa Kemal had his Headquarters. The attack on the Sharon Plain was left to the remaining infantry and was the main target of the cavalry. There were three divisions of Cavalry. The Australian 3rd Brigade under Major Olden and the 4th and 5th Divisions composed mainly of Indians under Lieutenant General Barrow. The 10th was the vanguard of the attack.

Herman sat on the stubbly ground of the Plain of Sharon. The hot summer had baked the earth and only memories of the winter crops remained. He sat under the muzzle of his horse and drank a mug of tea. "Steady boy," he said as the first cannon blast received a snort of approval from his faithful companion. The men of the 10th were unusually quiet except for Tex Morton who snored peacefully.

After fifteen minutes the Allied Infantry began to traverse the five miles between them and the enemy lines. The September sun sent shafts of light across the Judean Hills colouring them red.
"Red sky in the morning, shepherd's warning," Herman muttered to himself.

"Do you believe that?" asked Mick Foley on his right.

"It works for me," said Jack Clare on Herman's left. They watched the infantry proceed under the fire of rifle and machine gun. Men fell but the waves kept moving forward.

"The infantry are bloody tough," Barry Clay observed, taking his dentures from his mouth and putting them in his saddlebag.

At 6.30 am the whistle was blown indicating the order to mount up and so began the ride that was to last thirteen days and nights and cover a distance of 250 miles over some of the most perilous terrain in the world with narrow passes and sheer cliffs and ruthless plains. They would encounter 100,000 Turks. They would fight some twenty battles and skirmishes and end up in Damascus where they would meet victory and malaria. Truly, during the war Herman Murphy rode a horse.

Herman slipped into the saddle and patted Peter his horse on the neck. "Another day down on the farm old son," he said soothingly. He then turned to Socks who was standing besides him. "Chin up, beautiful one," he encouraged.

"Neigh," responded Socks.

In a line stretching for almost a mile, the 10th moved forward. They followed the 4th and 5th Mounted Divisions. The men had a bandoleer of ninety rounds over their shoulders and one around their neck. Their rifles were in their saddle holsters. In their hands they carried a two-edged sabre. They commenced at a walk. The ground was covered with the stubble from the winter crops. At the edge of each paddock was a small gutter used for irrigation. It was dry. The occasional olive grove added a little colour to the grey and brown fields. They weaved their way through the six-foot high cactus fences.

Some 300 yards from the first line, Major Olden gave the order. "On the trot." The roll of thunder came from the horse's hooves as they kicked up clouds of menacing dust. The infantry had cut the wire or pushed it down with whatever could be found, wooden doors, sand bags, and corrugated iron. The horses cleared the first line.

"Good on ya mate," the infantry, shouted at the horsemen.

The horsemen galloped on to the second line. With the sound of thundering hooves and the flash of cold steel approaching them, the Turks either ran or thrust up their hands in surrender. The infantry took the prisoners and the 10th moved on. The Turks withdrew into the redoubts around the towns, but the cavalry soon made short work of these.

The cavalry moved north along the coast taking the small towns. At the end of the Plain of Sharon, rose the Range of Mt Carmel. Once the hills of Mt Carmel were secured the cavalry moved through the Musmus Pass. This was difficult to find and one of the regiments of the 4th Division missed the pass and continued on for four miles. When they realised their mistake and retraced their path and found the pass, the Commanding officer, Lieutenant General Barrow was so angry he immediately demoted the officer in charge of the regiment.

As they passed through Musmus, the leading regiment came upon the squadron of Turks who was guarding the pass. The Turks had chosen to guard the pass at the exit instead of the entrance. They were caught napping. They were sitting around a campfire drinking apple tea and singing songs. Their rifles were neatly piled up several yards from their friendly sing along. The one hundred surprised Turks immediately surrendered.

Passing by Mount Megiddo in the evening of the 19th and early morning of the 20th, the Cavalry reached the Plain of Esdraelon. Directly across the plain from the Musmus Pass sitting snugly in the foothills of Lower Galilee was Nazareth.

Nazareth was the headquarters of Otto Liman von Sanders, the commander of the 7th Turkish Army. As all communications were cut to his headquarters and as the Australian Mounted Division moved so rapidly, he was still in his pyjamas when the cavalry mounted their attack on Nazareth. He hurriedly packed his papers and slipped into his Mercedes and while still in his pyjamas narrowly escaped. He left behind a lorry loaded with 20,000 pounds worth of gold sovereigns and a lorry of champagne both of which were guarded by a bear, which put up more fight than the Turks at that time of morning.

Outside Nazareth, Major Maloney directed. "A cadence gentlemen."

To the sounds of *Waltzing Matilda* the Aussies passed through the hometown of Jesus. Herman pulled rein next to a local shopkeeper. He spoke in Arabic.

"What did you say?" asked Mick Foley when Herman re-joined the troop.

"I asked him did he know any good carpenters around here," replied the tired, but still cheeky trooper. Herman and his mates checked out the carpentry shop but decided they could not carry a beautifully carved cabinet made from cedar, so they decided to move on. By lunchtime they were at the hillside town of Afula. This town was about eight miles from Nazareth and it had an airstrip used by the German Air force. Herman and his companions were several miles ahead of the main column. The airstrip was on the outskirts of the town.

"Well looky here," said Herman as he pulled rein. "I think we have an airstrip that does not know there is a war going on."

The ten troopers dismounted leaving their mounts under the cover of several olive trees, behind an abandoned shed. They secretively walked up to the main building with fixed bayonets. This building was divided into three sections. In the centre was the administration block; on one side was the mechanics' mess, on the other was the officers' mess.

"Could you book me a flight to Australia?" asked Maurice Quirke as he entered the administration centre. Dutchie Holland, Tex Morton and Basil Hickey followed him.

The German soldiers simply raised their hands. They were ushered into the Officers' Quarters where Jackie Clare, Herman Murphy, Mick Foley and Remo Genetti were seated comfortably in the lounge chairs around a casual table. Three German officers sat demurely in the corner. Maurice Quirke entered followed by the clerical staff and his smiling comrades.

One of the officers said arrogantly. "I demand to see your commanding officer. I am an officer of the German Army and demand the respect an officer should receive from the enlisted men."

'Shut your gob, mate," Maurice said courteously. "You're just the enemy to me."

Barry Clay, minus his teeth, with Jack Ryan, John O'Halloran and Brendan Duffy brought in the mechanics and ground crew.

"I reckon there is lunch somewhere around here," said Remo Genetti and he began looking for a cellar, which he found. A trap door into the underground cellar revealed a large quantity of vintage wine and champagne. Remo got assistance from Brendan Duffy, Tommy O'Farrell and John O'Halloran. The German chef served the Australians a delicious meal of cabbage and sausage.

A lorry pulled up outside and two German soldiers entered carrying a strong box.
"G'day mate. Come and have lunch," was the welcome they received from the toothless grin of Barry Clay. Jack Ryan opened the strong box revealing a pay roll of some 2000 gold sovereigns.
"English currency," said Jack.
"Bloody Beauty," responded the troopers. "Spoils of war."
The wine was drunk and the sovereigns mislaid.

Lieutenant Hans von Fickler was in the air over the Jordan Valley. He and his two companions had fired their thousand rounds into the Anzac Mounted Rifles as they pushed towards Amman. They had been in the air for three hours and returned to base in the Plain of Esdraelon. They landed their planes on the small airstrip of Afula.
"The ground crew will be on report when I see them," he said angrily and stormed off into the officers' mess.
"Come in mate," was the welcome he received. When a squadron of the 4th division caught up, the unhappy band of German airmen was delivered into their hands. The Aussies moved on, a little wobbly in the saddle. No one ever found the payroll.

AWM Collection Record: H02823

Fig. 22. Aircraft at Afule.

Chapter 24: On to Damascus

The troops of the Mounted Division moved through the Jezreel Valley. It is poorly drained by the River Kishon which zigzags across the valley. This is the home of mosquitoes. The fertile valley was filled with orchards of all kinds of fruit. Even in the battle conditions enterprising farmers proffered their goods to the passing parade of cavalry. "Best bloody orange I've ever tasted," said Paul Flanagan as he munched on his orange. Juice ran down the sides of his mouth making little valleys through his mud caked face.

During the course of the day the Mounted Division met resistance at the small towns in the Jezreel Valley. In addition to Nazareth and Afula they also took Jenin and Beisan (Beth shean). The 10th regiment took up residence in Jenin for a couple of days. While the cavalry had secured the Plain of Sharon and the Plain of Esdraelon beyond the Mt Carmel Hills, Chetwode and his infantry divisions had been equally successful in taking Nabulus the city in the Judean Hills where Mustafa Kemal had established his headquarters. Kemal managed to escape by car along the road that led from Nablus to Damascus. His command the Turkish Seventh Army, attempted to retreat east directly across the Jordan.

On September 21st, the allied aircraft spotted a large column of Turks in a defile west of the Jordan River. Continuous air attacks destroyed the defile. Not many soldiers died but transport and artillery and heavy equipment were abandoned and the survivors scattered leaderless. Over the next four days the Fourth Mounted Division and the Australian Mounted Division rounded up large numbers of demoralised and disorganised Turkish troops in the Jezreel Valley and Esdraelon Plain. The members of the 4th Mounted Division were Bengal Lancers and speaking in Hindustani contributed to the fear of the Turkish soldiers.

Allenby ordered the 3rd Indian Infantry to move north along the coast towards Beirut and the 7th Indian Division to move northeast to Baalbek. Their plan was to take Homs and Aleppo and cut off the Turkish retreat further north to Constantinople. Allenby ordered his cavalry to cross the Jordan and capture Amman, Deraa and Damascus. Chaytors' Anzac Mounted crossed the Jordan and on the 26th of September secured Amman and the Turkish 4th Army finding itself cut off from retreat, surrendered to the Anzacs rather than risk being slaughtered by the Arab irregulars.

Otto Liman von Sanders, after being unceremoniously driven from Nazareth, had established his headquarters at Samakh. This small fishing village on the southern shores of the Sea of Galilee had a population of 1,000 people. With the arrival of the Turks, the population increased by 5,000 soldiers. The Yarmuk River fed into the Jordan River about five miles from the southern tip of the Sea of Galilee. Otto Liman von Sanders had attempted to hold the line of the Jordan and Yarmuk rivers around the Sea of Galilee. He had his troops form redoubts on the southern sides of the rivers and trenches about one mile around the rim of Samakh which was just east of the Jordan River on the Junction of roads from the west and the east and the south and the north.

At 4.30 am on the 26th of September, the 10th Regiment slipped into their saddles. "Let's move quietly into the dawn," said Major Maloney as the men rode single file from the town of Jenin. The cavalry moved across the Plain of Esdraelon and entered the finger of the Jesreel Valley. As they moved through the villages, they were offered the produce of this fertile valley. Oranges, peaches, apricots, almonds and of course dates. They collected members of the Mounted Division as they progressed and stopped at the town of Betshean. Here they rested and took cover from the mid day sun. By mid-afternoon they reached the Jordan River, which was wide and deep and in this location moved quite rapidly. Scouts found a relatively narrow shallow section. The horses entered the water which felt cold after the hot ride.

When they reached midstream the men slipped from the saddle and swam beside their horses. The banks were slippery as they exited the river and assembled on the east bank. The men removed the saddles and rubbed their mounts down until they were dry. Their own clothes however remained wet.

Fig.23. Map of the Ride to Damascus

Otto Liman von Sanders had been born into the Prussian aristocracy on February 17, 1855. He had been appointed to the Ottoman Empire as a military adviser but he had little faith in the Turkish soldier. The German Commander sat on the balcony of the three-storey villa he had taken as his headquarters. He surveyed his lunch of unleavened breads and varietal salads, bowl of fruit and freshly grilled fish. He sipped discontentedly on his reserve champagne saved by his aide de camp when they had hurriedly left Nazareth. He cursed the heat and the inefficiency that surrounded him. He took up his binoculars and looked at the entrenchments along the Jordan and Yarmuk rivers.

Once again his faced drained as he watched the dribble of cavalry moving on the east bank of the Jordan River. He saw them stop and take up positions for a bayonet charge.

"Will they never stop?" he muttered to himself.

Rather than a mounted charge, the 10th had elected to make it a bayonet charge. The horses were tired. First at the walk and then at the full run with blood curdling yells, the men charged. They leapt into the trenches and went into action. White flags appeared. Otto Liman had left the building.

As the tired horsemen moved through the town they sang their signature song. They reached the banks of the Sea of Galilee and washed away the grime of the battle. That night they rested around campfires and enjoyed a fish supper.

Lawrence with his Arabs was moving along the Hejaz line. Lawrence captured the Rail Junction at Deraa and discovered that the Turks had treated resisting Arab villages badly so the Arab group took no prisoners as they moved forward. An entire Turkish brigade (along with some German and Austrians) was massacred near the village of Tafas on September 27th with the Turkish commander Jemal Pasha narrowly escaping. The Arabs repeated this performance the next day, losing a few hundred casualties while wiping out nearly 5,000 Turks in these two battles.

The Golan Heights Plateau bounds the eastern side of the Sea of Galilee. It is 690 square miles in area and rises from 400 feet above sea level to 1,700 feet above sea level. It is bound on the north by a range of mountains the highest of which is Mount Hermon. Here the transfiguration of Jesus occurred. In the south is the Yarmuk River. This plateau is the water shed for the Sea of Galilee, the Yarmuk and the Jordan rivers. Its sweet volcanic soil makes it suitable for beef and dairy cattle as well as orchards and vineyards. On the morning of the 27th, the 10th as part of the Australian Mounted Division began its journey to Damascus.

"No one is to enter the city of Damascus until Sherif Feisal and his United Arab Army arrive. They are to be the first to enter the city," Allenby instructed his Egyptian Expeditionary Force.

The 5th Indian Mounted Division and the Australian Mounted Division moved quickly across the Golan Heights. As the cavalry moved forward, the Australian Flying Corps supported them. Among the pilots were P.J. McGuiness and William Hudson Fysh who later with ground engineer Arthur Baird started the Queensland and Northern Territory Aerial Services, commonly known as Qantas. These men had been Light Horsemen first and then joined the air force. As the cavalry moved across Golan Heights, they fought actions at Benat, Yakup, Kuneitra, Sasa and Katana on the plateau. Undeterred they moved relentlessly to Damascus. Von Sanders and Kemal realising that annihilation was inevitable, left Damascus placing an Arab Administration in charge. Kemal fled 200 miles to Aleppo to make a final stand. Von Sanders escaped to the coast and then to Malta where he was later captured.

The 3rd Brigade led by the 10th regiment was to circle clockwise north and north east of Damascus and close off the exits of Damascus to the City of Homs.

On the 30th of September, the Australians reached the Barada Ridge. The Barada Gorge was one hundred yards wide. The River Barada, fed by the Lebanon Mountains, flowed swift and deep.

"Cop that lot," said Barry Clay. "I think the whole Turkish and German army are out for a picnic."

The road and railway were packed with troops leaving Damascus. Every kind of vehicle was on the move. With machine guns loaded on the backs of lorries and rail cars, the Turks and Germans opened fire on the Australian Light Horse. But here the Australians had the high ground. The sides of the gorge were too steep for a mounted charge so the supporting machine gunners took control. With deadly accuracy the Australians picked off their targets. Explosions from within the city of Damascus and its surrounds could be heard as the fleeing Turks blew up their reserve fuel and ammunitions and artillery.

At 10.00 pm the men were ordered to bivouac for the night on the Barada Ridge. It was a simple matter: unsaddle your horse, tether it to the saddle, roll up in your greatcoat and go to sleep. It was not a quiet night. The Turks periodically fired into the surrounded ridges from the cluttered gorge. Amidst the Australians that night was Lawrence and his Arab volunteers.

At 4.00 am Tuesday the 1st of October the men of the 3rd Brigade with the 10th regiment as the vanguard were in the saddle. They moved down the southwest of the Barada Gorge and across the open plain to Damascus. Their orders were to stop the enemy escaping along the Homs Road by circling northeast and not to go through the city, but as the Barada Gorge was blocked with escaping soldiers, dead soldiers, wounded soldiers, trucks, carts and cannon and the way to the north was too mountainous, Brigadier General L.C. Wilson, commander of the 3rd Brigade, decided to take a short cut through the city. Instead of circling the city, they headed straight for the southwest gate. With drawn sabres, they began their charge as soon as they reached the levels.

Nine hundred men all from Western Australia charged. The thunder of the hooves, the clink of the saddlery, the cannon shots and the rat tat of the machine guns with the intermittent rifle shot, rose in a cacophonous sound of terror, fear, anger and exhilaration as the men rode in a pall of dust to the oldest city on earth. Some 800 men entrenched outside the city provided resistance but as the 10th drew closer, the fear of cold steel weakened the enemy's resolve. They dropped their weapons, raised their hands and surrendered. As the tired horsemen reached the gates, the citizens with baskets of fruit, cigars, cakes and unending jubilation greeted them.

"Bloody dusty ride," said Maurice Quirk. "I could do with a beer." "Looks a bit like Geraldton," Herman said and his companions laughed in relief. As they rode through the dirty streets they could see no grandeur.

"Not much of a city," said Paul Flanagan.

The Capture of Damascus - 1918

***Fig. 24. 10th Regiment Australian Light Horse ride into Damascus at
7.30 am 1st October, 1918***

They passed the military parade grounds and the city garrison of
10,000 Turks in full parade saluted them. When they turned into
Government Street that led to the Serai (the Town Hall), they were
astounded by the sights of grandeur that greeted them.

"Wow," they gasped. Here were the lawns and gardens, steps and
marble, fountains and obelisks. Major Olden, Commander of the 10th
Regiment, called a halt outside Government House. He dismounted
and with two other men entered the town hall to claim the city. With
a revolver in each hand he climbed the sweeping stairs flanked by
guards and entered a vast, airy, high ceilinged, gaudy salon. It was
6.00 am.

"Where's the Governor?' he asked.

"He awaits you in the hall above," the interpreter replied.

Wearing a dark suit and a tarboosh, the small man who had been
appointed, temporarily, the Governor of Damascus sat in a plush

golden chair. Emir Said al Jeairi was an Arab. Olden stopped in the middle of the room.

"Tell him to get out of his chair and come and talk to me here," Olden said.

Gracefully Emir Said accommodated the major.

"In the name of the City of Damascus I welcome you, the first of the British Army."

"Does the city surrender?" Olden asked.

'Yes, there will be no further opposition in the city."

'Well what is all that firing in the streets?" Olden asked.

"It is our people welcoming you," was replied.

"Tell them to stop because we might mistake the intent of the discharging of a weapon."

Emir issued an order to a guard who immediately disappeared to stop the celebratory firing of the rifles. Emir Said began a long flowery speech in Arabic.

"Tell him to stop," said Olden." I am here to take the city on behalf of my commander Brigadier Allenby. He can give his speech then. Tell him I need his assurance that order will be maintained in the city."

"I guarantee that the rifles will be quietened and order will be maintained. Would the major care for some refreshments?" continued Emir Said.

"Thank you. No. I will rejoin my men. May I remind you that the city is surrounded." He turned on his heels and returned to his men. He mounted his horse and at the walk proceeded towards the Homs Road.

It was like a triumphal march through the city. Flowers, confetti, sweets were thrown to the soldiers as they passed. The men and women hugged them.

"Bit of a fuss," said Dutchie Holland.

"It's the posh soap you've been using," said Jack Clare as he enjoyed a rather large cigar.

The men exited the city and bivouacked along the Homs Road.

Lawrence woke at 6.00 am. He shaved and dressed in the clothes of a Sheik which he bragged cost him 200 pounds. In his armoured blue Rolls Royce, he made his way to Damascus. On the outskirts of the city, Indians of the 4th Division stopped him.

"No Arabs are allowed in," the Sergeant of Arms said in perfect Hindustani. After a long delay Lawrence eventually had himself identified as a British Officer. He entered the city in his car at 9.30 am. He later declared how he entered in glory on a horse but this was not the case. Lawrence tended to fantasize a little. His entry was somewhat of an anticlimax unidentified by the surrounding throng. The real heroes had passed through three hours before.

For the rest of the day the 1st the 3rd Brigades celebrated. Even the horses drank champagne and ate grapes and dates. The men of the 10th were running on adrenalin.

Allenby drove from his headquarters in Tiberias, a journey of eight hours but only a distance of 120 miles as the crow flies. He arrived on Thursday 3rd of October. Chauvel had organised a guard of honour for Allenby's triumphal entry into Damascus. The Desert Mounted Column provided the guard of honour. Lieutenant General, the Emir Feisal came by train from Deraa and instead of getting into a car and driving through the gates of Damascus he mounted a white horse and entered at the gallop amidst cheers from the welcoming crowd at 3.00 pm in the afternoon.

Allenby arrived several minutes later and went to the Hotel Victoria for a meeting with his general staff. He had no time to waste. He needed to settle Damascus and return to Tiberias to monitor the final stages of the campaign against the Turks.

Despite delightful and courteous circumventure of the truth on the side of Lawrence and Feisal it was agreed that Feisal would set up a government for the city of Damascus with a French adviser. As Lawrence said he could not operate this way, it was suggested he take long service leave, so he did. He was twenty-nine years of age.

By the 5th of October Damascus was in a shambles. Looting, rioting and murder were rife. In addition basic civil services were neglected. The Desert Mounted Column, having fought through four hundred miles of the roughest terrain in the Middle East, now bivouacked on the out skirts of the city was being attacked by mosquitoes carrying malaria and Spanish influenza.

"Shit Murph. You don't look too good," said Mick Foley who looked across at his mate mid afternoon of the 5th of October.

"Catch him," cried Maurice Quirke as Herman fell forward onto his horse's mane, turned and would have fallen to the ground if Mick had not grabbed his bandoleer. His mates took him to a make shift tent.

"He needs to see a doc," said Jack Clare.

"We're not taking him to the hospital. He'd be dead in a day in that filthy hole they call a hospital," Dutchie Holland urged. So the men of tent 13 and 14 looked after their mate. For four days Herman journeyed in a malarial fever. He fought monsters and bathed in blood. He ran across fields and sheared barbed wire sheep. He fed on horses' entrails and talked with headless men who ran around squirting blood into the air and then on the 9th of October he opened his eyes and saw the cheeky grin of Paul Flanagan looking at him. "Bloody shit Murph we thought you were a gonna," was the concerned comment.

As the mist of the fever left the trooper he began to come back to reality. "How's Pete?" he asked. "That's fine" Maurice Quirke complained. "We took it in turns to keep you bloody alive and all you think of is your bloody horse."

Everyone wanted to bring the big farmer up to date.

"We lost Dutchie. Same as you only went to bed with a fever. He was dead in the morning. I think we've lost more men from the mozzies than from the Turks. We need to get out of this hell hole," said Jack Clare as he fed Herman vegetable soup.
"The 5th division has gone charging up the Homs Road chasing after Liman von Sanders and Kemal," added Paul Flanagan.
"Those Indians don't give up easily," replied Herman.
"The rest of the cavalry units are too depleted by this bloody flu to go anywhere," piped in Brendan Duffy.

From the 5th to the 12th of October, admissions from the Desert Mounted Corps to the hospital in Damascus doubled from 1,246 to 3,109. The conditions were horrendous. Nearly four times the number of horsemen died in the crammed unhealthy dormitories of Damascus than had died on the advance.

Allenby returned to Tiberias. He wanted to keep pushing the Turk out of the Middle East. Kemal moved along the Homs Road burning and destroying anything he thought the advancing Egyptian Expeditionary Force could use. At Ridyak, the small railway town some 25 miles north of Damascus, he destroyed the railway station. Ridyak was the terminus of the train line that ran all the way to Constantinople. He also destroyed the waterworks. He then moved to Aleppo burning and destroying installations as he went. Thousands of Turkish troops remained behind to be taken prisoner.

Finally the remaining troops of the 4th Turkish Army were combined with the 7th Turkish Army and Kemal took complete charge. He set up his headquarters in the Baron's Head Hotel in Aleppo. On the 15th of October, the 5th Desert Mounted Corps with Arab detachments entered the city. Kemal left and set up resistance with his last remaining troops at Mouslimmive, just north of Aleppo. On the 25th and 26th, he directed his troops to fight the British and Arab forces. He drove the British back. He was prepared to defend the motherland to the last man. But other factors were at play.

The 3rd Indian Infantry had already taken Beirut on the 8th of October and the 7th Indian division occupied Baalbek on the 12th of October so the Coastal regions were in British hands.

Across the Mediterranean Sea, the Allies broke through the Turkish Western Front at Salonika in Greece. Turkey was now surrounded. On the 30th of October 1918, Vahideddin, signed the armistice on board the British cruiser *Agamemnon*. Vahideddin was the representative of the Sultan of the Ottoman Empire, Mehmed the Sixth. The terms were dictated by the Commander in Chief of the Mediterranean fleet, Sir Somerset Gough Calthorpe. The first clause of the twenty-four articles of the Turkish armistice was for the opening of the Dardanelles and the Bosphorus and the Black Sea. It also provided for the allied occupation of the Dardanelles and the Bosporus forts. Within two weeks of signing the armistice, the British sailed through the Narrows to Constantinople.

What had been planned to take a week had taken 300 weeks.

Chapter 25: Shores of Tripoli

Herman moved uncomfortably under his greatcoat. It was the 1st of November 1918. He slept with his feet pointing towards the dying coals of the campfire around which he and his companions had spent the night. It was one of the many campfires dotted along the road to Homs. The 10th Australian Light Horse Regiment had resided here since taking Damascus almost a month previously. He sat up and looked across the small cocoons of greatcoats that contained his tired mates, to his horse standing loyally under a palm. He gave a soft whistle. The horse whinnied acknowledgement. He kicked off his coat, stood up, stretched, collected the billy and walked to the food wagon. Here he filled the billy with water and returned to his campfire. He stirred the coals and threw new dry logs on the fire, which sprang to life. He hung the billy over the fire and then went to his horse. He filled the water trough and hung the nosebag filled with oats over the horse's head.

"Here you are, Uncle Toby's rolled oats for breakfast," he joked with his horse, Peter.

Socks grunted a complaint so Herman proceeded to attend to his mates' horses. When he returned, Kev Morton was awake and had put tea in the billy.

"Good morning, Ahmed," greeted Tex using Herman's nickname. Herman had earned the name Ahmed because he could communicate to the Arabs in an Australian style of Arabic.

"Good morning, Tex," Herman returned the greeting a little surprised to see Tex awake. "Couldn't sleep mate?"

"I had a great sleep," Tex replied as he poured a mug of tea, and warmed himself by the fire. Soon their mates joined the couple and sleepy conversations punctuated with long pauses began. By mid morning the men had breakfasted, attended to their horses and were sitting around in groups chatting.

Major Maloney walked over to his squadron.

"Gentlemen, I want trooper Murphy, Clare and Quirke to mount their horses and ride into town and acquisition whatever is needed. No! I countermand that order. I want all of you to go to town and acquisition whatever is need for a celebratory party. Turkey has surrendered!"

The spontaneous cry of joy resounded through the camp. A flock of pigeons took flight and all the hens laid an extra egg.

"With speed," Major Maloney called after his men as they galloped into Damascus. This time the swords were sheathed.

Within two hours the small troop had returned followed by three carts laden with the supplies. Joy is a spontaneous thing. It had a healing effect as it spread through the roadside residence of the 3rd Brigade.

From unknown places several footballs appeared. Makeshift cricket bats were created. The Australians and New Zealanders celebrated as one. The Arabs, Indians, French and English endeavoured to join in but considered the games the Anzacs played were more dangerous than the war just fought. At dusk a combined service was held which included Christian, Muslim, Hindu, Buddhist and Jew to thank the God of their belief for the peace that had arrived. Around the hundreds of night fires the men sang into the night, and then they slept and dreamt of home.

The 10th Regiment was among the many Light Horse Regiments that travelled along the Homs Road next morning. They were heading for Tripoli on the coast. The journey was slow and easy. Despite the cold and the rain and the poor condition of the road, which had been traversed by the traders for almost three thousand years, it was like a road to paradise with home at the end of it. The men changed *Marching through Georgia* to *Marching to Tripoli* and sang with great gusto. They then sang *Waltzing Matilda.* This was followed by a whole variety of songs with unrepeatable lyrics.

"There she blows," shouted Herman as he sighted the blue Mediterranean Sea from the crest of the hills of Lebanon.

A royal welcome greeted the victorious troopers as they rode through Tripoli, so named by the ancient Greeks because of the Triple cities of Tyre, Sidon and Arados. "I'm not going home. I am going to settle here," sighed Paul Flanagan as a young lady kissed him. Barry Clay had his teeth in and captured the hearts of a many a lady that day.

Tent city was in the village of Medjelaya some three miles south of the out skirts of Tripoli. The men enjoyed a meal of lamb on the spit with potatoes in the coals of the campfire. The tea was boosted with a double issue of rum.

"Since we are near the sea, we are virtually the navy so we have to follow their regulations," Kev Morton had suggested and heartily reissued himself with another round of rum. It was the 9th of November 1918.

"We should be home by Christmas," Paul Flanagan yawned as he pulled his greatcoat up to his chin, that night.
"What will happen with our horses?" asked Mick Foley.
"We take them home with us," replied Herman and silence fell over the camp as darkness put out the lights of the day.

Chapter 26: Germany Surrenders

The Turkish defeat hastened Germany into signing its own armistice in France on the 11th of November 1918.

Being at the top of the line of tents in the tent city the occupants of tent 13 and 14 were the first to hear the news. Chaos ruled supreme. First the men hugged each other and then they ran frantically from tent to tent screaming:

"It's over! It's over!"

"Permission granted," replied Major Maloney to the request from his squad to go to town and celebrate.

As he saw them disappear in a cloud of dust, he thought to himself. "This is the first time those larrikins have asked my permission to do anything," he followed the lads into town and celebrated with them. Even in celebration, the 10th was always controlled and respectful of fairness. However, their horses brought them home that night as they were in no condition to direct anything.

Cavalrymen always have a regular routine to keep their bodies busy and their minds away from real thinking. They had to groom and feed their horses. They had to maintain their weapons and saddlery. There were questions, however, which were continually coming into their minds, being asked but never answered.

"When are we going home and can we take our horses with us?"

"We all can't go at once," suggested Paul Flanagan as he poured water into the water trough. It was the 10th of December 1918.

"I haven't heard of any going yet," added Jack Clare. "I don't mind. They are paying me for nothing. I'd be crutching sheep back home. Shit of a job."

All laughed because roughly that was what crutching meant namely, cutting the shit off the sheep's backside, or in upper class circles *'removing the dag.'*

Not all the Light Horse went to Tripoli. Several brigades went to Ludd, which is seven miles directly east of Jaffa. Some of the troopers were located in Richon le Zion, a Jewish settlement, two miles south of Ludd. The local Arabs were constantly stealing from the camp. Complaints to the local authorities were ignored. The situation came to a head on the 10th of December.

Just after midnight, twenty one year old Kiwi Trooper Leslie Lowry's kit bag, which he was using as a pillow, was snatched from under his head. Lowry ran out of the tent to confront the thief who shot him in the chest and killed him. When the soldiers woke, they saw the tracks leading from their dead mate towards the local Arab village of Surafend. They went and confronted the villagers, demanding that they give up the thief. At the same time, they watched a group of villagers leave. The village elder said the killer had left the village, and spat in anger at the soldiers. The New Zealanders returned to their camp, but when the military police refused to retaliate, they rounded up a few Aussies and some Brits and raided the village. The soldiers went in with bayonets, pick handles and iron wrapped in sacking. They moved all the women and children out of the village, and beat about forty men to death. They then burnt their houses. The women and children returned to their ruined homes and dead loved ones.

Upon hearing of the massacre General Allenby called a general parade. Here he confronted the Anzacs. Ashamedly Major General Edward Chaytor stood and heard the commanding officer attack his beloved New Zealand Mounted Rifles.

"I was proud of you as brave soldiers, but now I am ashamed of you as cold blooded murderers," roared Allenby. He clicked his heals and withdrew. He confined all military personnel to tent lines. He cancelled the honours list for the Australian Light Horse and the New Zealand Mounted Brigades. He moved the camp to Rafah and had the British soldiers rebuild the destroyed homes in the village. He charged the New Zealand Government 858 pounds and the Australian Government 515 pounds.

For the 10th Australian Light Horse, however, spirits were quite high because on the 12th of December they moved from the mud of Medjelaya to the beach. Here in the soft warm sand they could escape the cold and enjoy a daily swim with their horses and mates. The lice, thankfully, found the environment not conducive to their way of life and left. The men were clean, happy and active again.

Chapter 27: A Last Sorrowful Ride

Christmas arrived with the Red Cross parcels so it was a time to celebrate *'Peace on Earth to Men of Good Will'*. The 10th celebrated around a giant Christmas tree decorated with shells, jam tins and seaweed. A united religious service was followed by carols and several extra rations of rum. On the 1st of January 1919, a race meeting was held on the beach. The horses relished the sand and enjoyed the cheering and the congratulatory embraces which followed a win or a loss.

Then came the worst news of all. The Horse Demobilisation Committee at the War Office issued a command that all horses were to be sold. There were over 22,000 horses that had fought side by side with their riders.

"These horses need better treatment," Herman argued. "I will pay for my horse to be transferred to Australia."

"No ships are available," responded Major Maloney. "We have to reinstate over a million troops to all parts of the planet."

"Have you seen how the locals treat their horses?" complained Maurice Quirke angrily.

"Orders are orders," replied Major Maloney. "The auction will take place at the end of the month. Orders from headquarters state that any horse lost will be immediately reported to British headquarters and within seven days a court of inquiry will be conducted."

As the sun set on the 29th of January, a small squadron of the 10th Regiment rode into the desert. Each man carried a shovel.

"Don't ask?" Herman snapped angrily at Peter who watched the trooper dig a large hole in the desert sand. A jackal barked in the distance. Herman removed the saddle from his faithful companion and threw it into the hole. He built a fire and boiled a billy then made a strong tea with many rations of rum.

"This is the end of the line old mate," he whispered to his horse as he placed a nosebag of fresh oats around his companion's neck.

Peter gave a deep understanding whinny and shook the nosebag free. He nuzzled his master. Herman stroked the neck of Peter. Herman closed down his emotions as he had done so often in the battles before and focused on the job to be done. He placed a handkerchief over the horse's eyes and led him to the edge of the hole he had dug some hours before. He placed the revolver to the centre of Peter's head and pulled the trigger. The sound of the weapon echoed through the night and through the soul of Herman as he watched his faithful companion fall into the hole, dead. With tears pouring down his cheeks he buried the horse and then walked back to the tent line. He reached the camp at first light and went to bed where he stayed for several days.

"Where are your mounts?" Major Maloney asked the men from tent 14 and 13.

"Wogs took 'em," was the united reply.

No Inquiry was conducted.

A race meeting was held on the 24th of February 1919, at the end of which 183 horses were led into an olive grove and given a nosebag of oats. After a half an hour marksmen shot the horses. Their hides, hair and flesh were sold. The men returned to the large common tent and received a lecture on *"Chinese and Japanese life and ideals."* Many could well ask what this had to do with the current reality of the men who had lost their equine war companions.

Chapter 28: Keeping the Peace

Keeping the peace was almost harder than winning the war. Allenby was responsible for maintaining order in Egypt, Sinai, Syria and Palestine. These lands came under the Occupied Enemy Territory Administration and Allenby was in charge.

The slowness of demobilisation was due primarily to Winston Churchill who had been appointed Secretary of State for War and Air. Where do they get these titles? Troops were stationed from Berlin to Jerusalem to enforce the terms of the peace.

On the 3rd of March 1919, the 10th Australian Light Horse boarded lorries with the rest of the 3rd Brigade. They were taken to the Port of Tripoli where they boarded the *SS Ellenga*. They arrived at Port Said on the 4th of March and travelled by train to Moascar where they handed in their weapons and sat around, waiting for transport home.

The Egyptians had been quiet during the war. They had resented being forced to work for the British for little pay. They were angry at not being represented at the Peace Conferences. Now they expected to be given self-rule but the British refused because the British needed the Suez Canal under British control. With all these grievances, the Egyptians rebelled.

"Egypt for the Egyptians," was their rebellious cry.

The Australian regiments were not sent home. They were reissued with weapons and new mounts and were required to keep the peace. Here Herman met up with his old mate, Andrew Barton Paterson, commonly called by his nickname Banjo Paterson.

Banjo Paterson had been a war correspondent in the Boer War in 1899. At the outbreak of war in 1914, he sold his property in Murrumbidgee and then obtained a position of honorary vet and travelled with the 7,882 horses with the first contingent of Australians to England. When he heard that a unit of men was being formed to train and care for horses in the Middle East he returned to Sydney, changed his birth date from the 17th of February 1864 to 1866, was accepted into the Remount Unit as a lieutenant and soon rose to the position of major. His unit comprised of twenty officers, three veterinary officers and 816 other ranks, which included blacksmiths, saddlers and wagon drivers. On the 8th of December 1915, he arrived on the *Orsova* at Port Said. He initially worked at Maadi camp. In March 1916 he was made the chief officer of the newly formed remount unit at the horse depot in the huge British base at Moascar just outside Cairo.

His squadron was made up of rough riders, jackeroos, horse breakers, buck jumpers and ex jockeys. '*The Man from Snowy River,*' a book of his poems including the legendary poem '*A Man From Snowy River*' was published in 1896 and was the most successful book of any kind published in Australia. Apart from Kipling, he had the biggest audience of any English poet.

On the 12th of March 1919, he stood with his foot resting on the lowest rail of a corral in Moascar Camp. He was talking to Herman.

"It is the greatest waste of horse flesh in recorded history," Andrew Barton Paterson complained. "Even Olden's two racehorses *Yahoo* and *Orchardor* were shot you say."

"I am afraid so," replied Herman noting that the treatment of the horses had so distressed his old mate that he was visibly ill.

"Well, what can we get for you, Ahmed?" he asked Herman, using Herman's nickname.

"The black will do nicely," replied Herman.

"His name is Jacko. You'll find him a good stayer. He'll go all day and night and then ask for more. I hope you won't have to shoot this one. It is too painful," Banjo said.

The treatment of the horses was too painful for Banjo who went on sick leave for several weeks and then sailed for Sydney on the 1st of April aboard the *SS Kildonan Castle*.

Herman collected the gelding and walked it to the Q store where he was issued with saddlery. He saddled his new horse and rode it into the desert west of Moascar.

He returned well into the night and tethered his horse on the line near his tent.

The coals in the fire were smouldering smokelessly, black and red. He stoked it and was soon joined by six of his mates, restless. "Can't sleep, Murph?" Maurice Quirke asked.

"Been for a ride," was the reply.

"I'll have a cup of that," said Jack Clare, rolling a smoke. The tea was shared. They conjectured about how long it would be before they went home. They discussed the way they could control the rebellious Egyptians. They talked about their new mounts. They talked about the officers. They were not happy little soldier boys.

Fearing insurrection from the Australians, the officers introduced incessant drill and route marches.

"Drill them! Drill them!" Allenby ordered. "There will be no insurgents in my ranks."

The Aussies went on strike.

Reveille blew. Drill sergeants were on the parade ground. They were alone.

"Shoot us if you like," said Jackie Ryan to Major Maloney. "We aren't doing any more stupid drill and senseless marches." The drill orders were countermanded. The Aussies were put on patrols to maintain order instead. They were the disorderly orderlies.

Eight British Officers and nurses were clubbed to death while on holiday in Luxor. The 10th did the 500 miles round trip to quell the riots. They found none. It was obviously the charisma of the 10th Australian Light Horse that brought peace to the area. When the 10th returned, they found there were constant demonstrations in the streets of Cairo and other larger towns. Railway lines and telegraph lines were constantly sabotaged. In Cairo itself the Armenians were targeted. Many were killed. The Young Turk Movement was blamed. But basically the Egyptians wanted independence and the British refused to allow this to happen. So the daily routine for the 10th was to do police patrols through the streets of Cairo and suburbs. However all was well in the Long Bar of the Shepheard's Hotel.

"Lieutenant! Another refill. There's a good fellow," Colonel Billingsworth spoke to the waiter. He was on his fourth gin and tonic and was speaking quite coherently.

"I say Jones, what is that commotion going on outside? I do believe it is a group of nuns in revolt."

"I don't think they are nuns, old chap. They are the Egyptian women dressed in the local attire. I believe they are calling for the liberation of the Egyptians from British rule," replied Colonel Mander Jones. "It'll never happen. These natives could never rule themselves. Ruling is a British thing," replied Colonel Billingsworth.

"Couldn't agree with you more. You don't think it could lead to another war old chap?"

"I very much doubt it, old chap. We have just had the war to end all wars," said Mander Jones as he sipped wisely on his gin and tonic.

"Your car awaits you, sirs," the young Lieutenant announced.

"Oh well back to jolly old England. It wasn't a bad war after all, don't you think?" commented Billingsworth philosophically.

"Yes! As wars, go it was quite good. Those colonials were a bit rough though," added Mander Jones as he stood somewhat gingerly.

"See ya mate," called Jack Ryan who was standing at the bar drinking a nice cold beer with his mates. "Don't forget to make sure your socks match your uniform."

"Yes of course," responded Mander Jones thoughtfully. "No couth. Absolutely no couth."

He walked out of the Shepheard's Hotel with his fellow Colonel. They boarded the car, which took them to a ship, which took them back to England where they would write their memoirs and make history.

As Napoleon commented:

'History is merely an agreed pack of lies.'

Chapter 29: Homeward Bound

On Sunday 6th of July a telegram came to Brigade Headquarters. Reveille was sounded. A short parade was held. "Gentlemen, I wish to inform you that you will all be expected to board the *SS Oxfordshire* on the 10th of July," announced the commanding officer. The men let out one almighty shout, which caused the officers in the Shepheard's Bar to spill their drinks even though it was ten miles away.

The men turned in their gear, packed their kit bag, marched to the station, travelled by train to Port Said and were walking up the gangplank in next to no time. There to farewell them was Allenby. He addressed his loyal soldiers for the last time.

"You the Australian Light Horseman have combined a splendid physique and restless activity of mind, rendering you somewhat impatient of rigid and formal discipline, but giving you the gift of adaptability mounted or on foot. Eager in advance and staunch in defence, you, the Australian Light Horseman have proved yourselves equal to the world's best, earning the gratitude of the Empire and admiration of the world. May you fare well and may we never have to fight such a conflict again."

"They can keep their Promised Land," said Paul Flanagan as he lent over the ship's rails.
The 10th was farewelled by an assortment of people.

There was still the cry of *'Egypt for the Egyptians'* resounding through the streets but this was no longer a concern of the soldiers. Their work was done and they were going home. As the *Oxfordshire* slowly made its way along the canal, the men bade farewell to the desert that had been their home for so long. Herman looked with sadness as he remembered his mates who were buried somewhere out there. In the corridors of his mind, he heard the morning whinny of Peter and the low growls of Socks. At dusk they reached the Red Sea.

The men were quartered in the holds of the ship. It was the middle of summer and they felt like potatoes in a cooking pot. Even on deck the air was so thick one could cut it with a knife and the steel of the decks turned into a frying pan. All was not bad however. The *Oxfordshire* also carried paying passengers and the sedate ladies and gentlemen added colour to life on board ship. Euchre tournaments were held. Bridge parties were organized. There were novels to read and magazines to look at. Added to this was the joy of going home and being free.

Shore leave was granted in Colombo. The plush jungles and greenery was a great contrast to the yellow sands of the desert. The men of tent 13 and 14 found a restaurant and enjoyed a delightful meal and sophisticated entertainment. It wasn't long before the boys began entertaining the locals. They sang *Waltzing Matilda, the Anzac Song, Marching though Georgia*. Paul Flanagan led the boys in a beautiful rendition of *Danny Boy*.

"You are always welcome. Come back as soon as you can," said the restaurant owner shaking their hands vociferously at the same time shaking his head in the customary way. As the ship left Colombo they were once again farewelled by the locals. Now it was straight home.

"Here's ten quid for the bloke who spots the Southern Cross first," challenged Jack O'Halloran in a sudden burst of passion. Night after night the boys watched the appearance of Venus and then the Big Dipper.

"Got it," shouted Kev Morton. "Thar she blows. *Beneath the Southern Cross we stand with a glass of beer in our hands. Australia! You bloody Beauty,"* good old Tex waxed poetic.

On the 1st of August, the first sightings of the Southern Cross put joy and hope in the hearts of the lads coming home from the war. This really assured them that the war was over and home was waiting for them.On the 4th of August the *Oxfordshire* berthed at Fremantle Harbour.

Iris stood on the wharf and scanned the ship. The rising sun caught Herman's ring and Iris's eye caught the reflection. Her heart gave a leap. Her man was home. She watched the men march down the gangplank. They stood in parade positions and were dismissed with six days leave. Herman searched the waiting crowd and there was Iris, his little flower. Next to her on crutches was Charlie Bunter. Herman was home. His war was over.

During the war he rode a horse but he also did a few other things.

Epilogue

Herman was discharged from the army on the 3rd of September 1919. He married his Iris and moved to Chalnooka, the family farm in the Chapman Valley. Here he built his home on a little hill some one hundred yards from his father's house. He had eight children. He worked the farm until World War Two was declared in 1939. He joined the army with his eldest son Sylvester Michael Murphy. Sylvester served in Darwin with the 2/16 and then moved to Egypt and Syria as his father had done in WW1. He returned to Australia when the Japanese threatened the continent. He served in New Guinea and was one of the heroic men of the Kokoda Trail.

Herman served at home at Rottnest Island. He was responsible for the planned evacuation of West Australia as the Japanese drew closer. Fortunately evacuation was never executed. After the war Herman moved his family to Maddington a suburb of Perth. He stayed in the army until 1956 when he retired. He then worked as an orderly in the Royal Perth Hospital until he retired in 1962.Iris died in 1970 and Herman died in 1972. Eight children, thirty-six grand children and seventy great grand children and ten great, great grand children lovingly remember him. He leaves behind a heritage of kindness, courage and tenacity.

Charlie Bunter did drive that lift in a leading ladies department store in Perth. It was always crowded. He had lost his legs but not his charm.

Bibliography

Aldington, R. *Lawrence L'Imposteur ('1955)*

Bean. C.E. *The Story of ANZAC.Volume One*. Sydney. Angus and Robertson. 1941. Pp 82-100.

Falls Cyril, *Armageddon, 1918*, J.B. Lippincott Company, 1964.

Grainger, John D. *The Battle for Palestine, 1917* (Woodbridge: Boydell Press, 2006) Retrieved from "http://en.wikipedia.org/wiki/Battle_of_Rafa"

Gullett, H.S. *The Australian Imperial Force in Sinai and Palestine: 1914—1918*, 10th edition, Angus and Robertson, Sydney, 1941, p. 221.

Gullett, H.S. *Official History of Australia in the War of '1914-1918—Sinai and Palestine, Vol. VII ('1923)*

Hamilton, Jill Duchess of. *First to Damascus the Australian Light Horse and Lawrence of Arabia*. Sydney. Kangaroo Press. 2002.

Hill,A.J. *Chauvel of the Light Horse : a biography of General Sir Harry Chauvel ('1978)*

James, J. *The Golden Warrior—The Life & Legend of Lawrence of Arabia* ('1995)

Jones,I. *The Australian Light Horse ('1987)*

Lawrence, T.E. *Seven Pillars of Wisdom—A Triumph ('1926)*

Liddell Hart, B. H. *History of the First World War*, Pan Books Ltd. London, ISBN 0330233548

Massey, W.T. *Allenby's Final Triumph ('1920)*

Maude, R. *The Servant, the General and Armageddon*, George Ronald Pub Ltd; ISBN 0-85398-424-7

Mitchell,E. *Light Horse, Chauvel Country: the story of a great Australian pioneering family* ('1978)

Olden, A. *Westralian Cavalry—10th Light Horse Regiment in the Great War '1914-1918* ('1921)

Perrett B. *Megiddo 1918—the Last Great Cavalry Victory*, Osprey Military Campaign Series 61, Oxford: Osprey, 1999. ISBN 1-85532-827-5

Rickard, J. *(2 September 2007), Battle of Rafa, 9 January 1917*, http://www.historyofwar.org/articles/battles_rafa.html

Rickard, J. *(2 September 2007), First battle of Gaza, 26-27 March 1917,* http://www.historyofwar.org/articles/battles_gazaI.html

Rickard, J. (2 September 2007), *Battle of Beersheba, 31 October 1917*, http://www.historyofwar.org/articles/battles_beersheba.html

Rickard, J. (3 September 2007), *Action of El Mughar, 13 November 1917*, http://www.historyofwar.org/articles/action_el_mughar.html

Rickard, J. (3 September 2007), *Battle of Jaffa, 21-22 December 1917,* http://www.historyofwar.org/articles/battles_jaffa.html

Seal. G. *Inventing ANZAC*. St Lucia. University of Queensland Press.2004

Shepheard's Hotel (Cairo, Egypt). *Cairo and Egypt: A Practical Handbook for Visitors to the Land of the Pharaohs* Cairo: Shepheard's Hotel, ca. 1897-1917. http://www.sil.si.edu/ondisplay/nile-

Te Ara—*The Encyclopedia of New Zealand, updated 18-Sep-2007* URL: http://www.TeAra.govt.nz/1966/W/WarsFirstWorldWar191418/en

Tucker, Spencer. *The Great War: 1914-18 (1998)'*WARS—FIRST WORLD WAR, 1914-18', *from An Encyclopaedia of New Zealand, edited by A. H. McLintock, originally published in 1966.*

Wavell, P. *Allenby: Soldier and Statesman* ('1946)

Web Sites

Australians of Arabia. Peter Hogan. pete@kxol.com.au
http://www.kxol.com.au/aoa
Battle of al Mughar http://www.firstworldwar.com/battles/mugharridge.htm
10th Regiment Riding into Damascus.
http://www.lancers.org.au/site/light_horse.asp
Battle of Megiddo.
http://en.wikipedia.org/wiki/Battle_of_Megiddo_(1918)
Race to Damascus.
http://www.nzetc.org/tm/scholarly/tei-WH1-Came-t1-body-d23.html

Appendices:

Appendix One: Departure dates and transport ships

10th Light Horse Regiment	Formed in Western Australia October 1914 for the 3rd Light Horse Brigade. departed Fremantle *Mashobra* 8th February 1915
First Reinforcements	departed Fremantle *Surada* 17th February 1915
Second Reinforcements	departed Fremantle *Itonus* 22 February 1915
Third Reinforcements	departed Fremantle *Argyleshire* 19 April 1915
Fourth Reinforcements	departed Fremantle *Hororata* 26 April 1915
Fifth Reinforcements	departed Fremantle *Karoola* 25 June 1915
Sixth Reinforcements	departed Fremantle *Kanowna* 2 July 1915
Seventh Reinforcements	departed Fremantle *Anchises* 2 September 1915
Eighth Reinforcements	departed Fremantle *Hororata* 5 October 1915
Ninth Reinforcements	departed Fremantle *Themistocles* 13 October 1915
Tenth Reinforcements	departed Fremantle *Benalla* 1 November 1915

Eleventh Reinforcements	departed Fremantle *Mongolia* 23 November 1915
Twelfth Reinforcements	departed Fremantle *Borda* 17 January 1916
Thirteenth Reinforcements	departed Fremantle *Warilda* 16 February 1916
Fourteenth Reinforcements	departed Fremantle *Ulysses* 1 April 1916
Fifteenth Reinforcements	departed Fremantle *Surada* 16 May 1916
Sixteenth Reinforcements	departed Fremantle *Morea* 6 June 1916.
Seventeenth Reinforcements	departed Fremantle *Mongolia* 6 July 1916.
Eighteenth Reinforcements	departed Fremantle *Malwa* 31 July 1916.
Nineteenth Reinforcements	departed Fremantle *Mooltan* 28 August 1916.
Twentieth Reinforcements	departed Fremantle *Bakara* 4 November 1916.
Twenty First Reinforcements	departed Fremantle *Bulla* 22 January 1917.
Twenty Second Reinforcements	departed Fremantle *Clan MacCorquodale* 13 February 1917
Twenty Third Reinforcements	departed Fremantle *Karmala* 12 February 1917
Twenty Fourth Reinforcements	departed Fremantle *Morea* 26 February 1917

Twenty Fifth Reinforcements	departed Fremantle *Port Sydney* 22 May 1917
Twenty sixth Reinforcements	departed Fremantle *Port Lincoln* 30 June 1917
Twenty Seventh Reinforcements	departed Fremantle *Kyarra* 17 July 1917
Twenty Eighth Reinforcements	departed Fremantle *Commonwealth* 9 Nov. 1917
Twenty Ninth Reinforcements	departed Fremantle *Ormonde* 13 March 1918

Appendix Two

3rd Light Horse Brigade [Australian Mounted Division]
Formed Australia October 1914. Attached to New Zealand and
Australian Division December 1914—April 1915. Assigned to
Anzac Mounted Division March 1916. Attached to British Imperial
Mounted Division February 1917. Assigned to Australian Mounted
Division June 1917.

Subunits:

8th Light Horse Regiment October 1914 to past November 1918
9th Light Horse Regiment October 1914 to past November 1918
10th Light Horse Regiment October 1914 to past November 1918
3rd Machine Gun Squadron 3 January 1917 to past November 1918
3rd Signal Troop October 1914 to past November 1918
Commanders:
Brigadier General F. C. Hughes 17 October 1914 to 8 October
1915
Brigadier General J. M. Antill 8 October 1915 to August 1916
Brigadier General J. R. Royston August 1916 to 30 October 1917
Brigadier General L. C. Wilson 30 October 1917 to past November
1918

Campaigns:

Egypt: Defence of Egypt,
Gallipoli: Defence of Anzac Cove, Nek, Suvla Sari Bair, withdrawal
from Anzac Cove, *Sinai:* Romani, Sinai, Magdhaba, Rafah,

Palestine: First Battle of Gaza, Second Battle of Gaza, Third Battle of Gaza, Beersheba, El Mughar, Nebi Samwil, Jerusalem, Jericho, Es Salt, Megiddo-Sharon, Esdraelon Valley, Semarkh, Plateau, Damascus

Casualties
World War I

237 killed, 479 wounded

Commanding Officers of the 10th Light Horse Regiment.

Brazier, Noel Murray.
Scott, John Burns.
Abbott, Percy Phipps.
Nicholas, Clive Lanyon.
Todd, Thomas John.
Grimwood, Samuel Edward.
Olden, Arthur Charles Niquet.

Decorations:

1 VC, 1 CMG, 3 DSO 1bar, 1MBE, 9MC 1 bar, 15 DCM 1 bar, 15 MM, 3MSM, 48MID,
4 Foreign Awards.

Appendix Three

Herman John Murphy Service Record

Enlisted Oath to be taken by person being enlisted;

I *Herman John Murphy* swear that I will well and truly serve our Sovereign Lord and King in the Australian Imperial Force from the 19/6/16 until the end of the War, and a further period of four months thereafter unless sooner lawfully discharged, dismissed or removed therefrom; and that I will resist His Majesty's enemies and cause His Majesty's peace to be kept and maintained; and that I will in all matters appertaining to my service, faithfully discharge my duty according to law. SO HELP ME GOD.

Signed: *H.J. Murphy*

Taken and subscribed at Black Boy Hill in
The State of Western Australia.
This 19th day of June 1916 before me.
Signed by the attesting Officer: A Getty 2nd Lieutenant.

Description of Herman John Murphy on Enlistment.
Age 19 years 11 Months.
Height 5 feet 9 and a half inches.
Weight 156 Pounds.
Chest Measurement 37/33 inches.
Complexion Dark.
Eyes Brown.

Hair Black

Religious Denomination C of E

Statement of Service of No 3672 Murphy H. J.

Unit in which served	Promotion	Date From	To
74 Depot	Private	19/6/16	22/7/16
21/16 Reinforcement	Private	22/7/16	14/9/16
6/44	Private	14/9/16	1/10/16
5/43	Private	1/10/16	6/12/16
22 Depot	Private	6/12/16	17/2/17
10/51	Private	17/2/17	23/3/17
X Depot	Private	23/3/17	10/4/17
Depot Squadron	Trooper	10/4/17	16/4/17
1st Machine gun Squadron	Trooper	16/4/17	

Statement of Service Of No 3672 changed to No 26 Murphy H. J.
Embarked Fremantle on HMAT Port Lincoln 30/6/17. Disembarked Suez 6/8/17

Date	Activity
6/8/1917	Disembark *Port Lincoln* to Moascar. Acting Sergeant without extra pay.
12/8/17	Reverts to Trooper
27/8/17	Sick to Hospital Mumps. Ismailia
20/9/17	Dismissed from Hospital.
28/9/17	Taken on strength. Transferred to 3rd Machine gun Squadron
29/9/17	Taken on strength. To 3rd Brigade 3rd MG S 10th ALH Egypt Expeditionary Force. EEF. Moascar Camp
16/3/18	Rest Camp Port Said.
23/3/18	Sick to Hospital. Port Said.
13/4/18	Rest Camp Port Said.
29/4/18	To Moascar.
15/6/18	Taken on strength EEF.
5/10/18	Admitted to Damascus Hospital.
9/10/18	Transferred to Ludd Hospital
12/10/18	Transferred to Gaza. Hospital
13/10/18	Transferred to Kantara. Hospital
24/10/18	Marched in to Port Said Rest Camp.
9/11/18	Marched out to Moascar.
30/11/18	Rejoined EEF
18/1/19	Appointed Driver for Vice 1862. C Brown.
18/3/19	Transferred to work in Hospital in Moascar
22/3/19	Transferred to work in Hospital in Cairo.

15/5/19	Reverts to Trooper on the Evacuation of the hospital
19/5/19	Returns to Moascar.
7/6/19	Abbassia Vehicle driver.
10/7/19	Embarked on *HMAT Oxfordshire*.
4/8/19	Disembarked *HMAT Oxfordshire* at Fremantle, West Aust. List No 308.
3/9/19	Discharged. Medals received: Star Medal, British War Medal and the Victory War Medal.

Battles in which Herman John Murphy participated

Date	Battle
27/10/17—7/11/17	Gaza—Beersheba
13/11/17	El Mughar.
17/11/17-24/11/17	Nebi Samwill
7/12/17-9/12/17 and 26/12/17—30/12/17	Jerusalem
21/12/17—22/12/17	Jaffa
19/2/18-21/2/18	Jericho
24/3/18-25/3/18	Jordan Es Salt.
15/9/18-19/9/18	Sharon Plains (Megiddo)
19/9/18-25/9/18	Esdraelon Valley (Nazareth, Al Afuleh, Beisan, Jenin)
26/9/18	Samakh
27/9/18-30/9/18	Golan Heights (Benat Yakup, Kuneitra, Sasa, Katana)
1/10/18	Damascus

Glossary

Aussie mateship: Strong friendship based on trust

Australian Rules Football: A unique game of football played in Australia. Each team consists of eighteenplayers. These are placed strategically in rows of three across the field. The postions are called: Full forwards, half forwards, centre, half backs and full backs. Three men form the ruck and they are called the knock ruck, ruck rover and the rover.

The field is in the shape of an oval which measures roughly one hundred and twenty to one hundred and eighty yards long and one hundred yards wide. There are four goal posts at each end with the centre two being longer than the outer two. There is no cross bar. A goal is kicked when the ball is kicked between the centre two posts. The value of a goal is six points. If the ball is kicked between the outer posts only one point is scored. The game commences with the umpire bouncing the ball in the centre of the field and the opposing knock ruckmen endeavor to tap the ball to their rover of ruck follower. The ball is oval in shape and about twelve inches long and eight inches wide. The game is broken into four quarters. Today each quarter is 20 minutes long but previously the time varied from 30 minutes to 25 minutes. The first recorded game of Australian Rules was played between Greenough Flats and Champion Bay now known as Geraldton. The game took place in 1860.

Boans: The first department store in Perth Western Australia

Book maker's last:	A boot maker's model of the foot on which boots and shoes are made or repaired
C'arn :	A cheering term commonly used at Australian Rules football matches. Means 'come on'
Dob of the footy:	Dob means kick and footy is the Australian rules football. Friends stand some forty yards apart and kick the ball to each other.
Down Under:	Refers to Australia because of its geographical position
Golden Fleece:	This is a fleece of wool off a sheep's back. It was golden because wool brought Australia a lot of export money.
Gunny sack:	A sugar bag. A bag made of hessian thirty inches wide and one yard long. It was used for transporting sugar
Outhouse:	Outside toilet.
Stab pass:	A low short pass in which the ball is dropped to the ground and kicked on the rebound. It travels thirty yards at chest height.
Tippy run:	A game of cricket in which the batsman has to run when he hits the ball.
Torpedo punt:	Is a long kick in which the ball spirals though the air like a topedo. Generally the punt travels sixty to seventy yards
Two up:	A gambling game in which one player holds two pennies on his flat hand and throws the coins into the air. Players bet on whether the coins will show odds or evens when they land. Odds is when the faces of the coins are different and the evens are when they are the same.